DEAR PHILIP

Dear Philip

A diary of captivity,
Changi 1942-45

Freddy Bloom

THE BODLEY HEAD
LONDON SYDNEY
TORONTO

British Library Cataloguing
in Publication Data
Bloom, Freddy
Dear Philip.
1. World War, 1939–45—Prisoners and prisons, Japanese
2. World War, 1939–45—Personal narratives, American
I. Title
940.54′72′520934   D805.J3
ISBN 0–370–30345–8

Copyright © Freddy Bloom 1980
Printed in Great Britain for
The Bodley Head Ltd,
9 Bow Street, London WC2E 7AL
by Thomson Litho Ltd, East Kilbride
set in monophoto Ehrhardt
First published 1980

For Virginia and William

Editor's Note

The original diary was written in a hardback, lined notebook, the first few pages of which were used for the accounts of a little NAAFI store in the General Hospital run by Freddy Bloom and Mrs Graham White. The diary then takes over and fills the notebook to the very last page.

Obviously there was more time and space for the entries of the first few months. Later the pages were carefully rationed and so the entries became shorter and more succinct until towards the end they are almost in telegraphic form.

To clarify certain points and identify certain people Freddy Bloom has annotated here and there. Her annotations appear in square brackets.

Preface to a Diary

When Singapore fell to the Japanese on 15 February 1942, a young American newspaper woman and her husband were taken prisoner. They had been married just nine days before, on her twenty-eighth birthday.

As a British doctor serving with the Royal Army Medical Corps, he was sent to the military prisoner-of-war camp at Changi. She was interned in the Changi civilian prison.

The two of them were separated for the next three and a half years, and during that time she kept a diary in the form of a letter to her husband, Philip. He read it only when they were at last reunited towards the end of 1945. The diary was then put away with sundry documents and mementos, until it came to light again some thirty-five years later.

The diary is an account of one young woman's reaction to 'Camp Life', which I now find makes strange reading, for I was that woman all those years ago. The details are still vivid in my mind. Each corner of the Camp, each incident, is like a sharply focused photograph. I can still hear the sounds and smell the smells, and though I normally have a notoriously bad memory for names and faces, the people from Camp days are indelible. Here is no account of unmitigated suffering. The daily activities and concerns of the women are mostly just a busy-ness, with an almost frothy quality. Of course, there was hunger, disease, indignity, cruelty, fear and death. They are the basic ingredients of all concentration camps. They are an essential part of war stories and the tales of Man's inhumanity to Man, but in reality, over any length of time, fear is like a bad smell. One gets used to it. Nobody can live indefinitely in a state of sustained horror.

When I think of Dachau or Belsen, my mind shudders for I can think only of the unbelievable atrocities, but I now

(7)

suspect that even there, in those utterly intolerable conditions, inmates were probably deeply concerned if they lost a button, were constipated or broke a tooth. These are immediate worries. They are normal and ordinary and people are drawn, almost magnetically, to the normal, ordinary aspects of life even under the most abnormal circumstances. Perhaps it is because there is security and safety in the familiar? What is more likely is that we are what we are. We can do only what we can do. We must relate any new experience to what we have already experienced. Our standards are the results of the lives we have led; they are what we know and we cling to them. And so the women who were caught in Singapore had to be themselves.

Who were we? At the beginning there were just over four hundred of us. A large number were 'Mems', wives of the men who worked in administration and industry, of rubber planters, tin miners, and so on. There was a sizeable contingent of civilian nurses who had chosen to stay behind. The military nurses had been ordered to leave, given no choice, but there was nobody in Singapore with the authority to order civilian nurses to leave. Many felt that it was their duty to stay. Then there were some teachers, missionaries, a few members of the Salvation Army and a small group of old or infirm ladies who had simply been left behind.

The majority of the women were European, the term used for all Caucasians. Then there were the Chinese, Malay, Eurasians, and the Indians who were married to British men or came from British families. There were at least two Japanese wives. It was a mixed bag, a mainly British mixed bag that also held about half a dozen Americans.

Looking back, perhaps our greatest blessing was that, though our captors provided us with the minimum in benefits, they also imposed the minimum of restrictions. We were confined where they wanted us to be confined. The space was insufficient but we could do more or less what we wanted

(8)

within it. They sent in a certain amount of food. They laid down a few rules. Then we were told to get on with it and make whatever we could out of the situation. Occasionally we annoyed them and they would give vent to their annoyance. On the whole, how we survived and whether we survived or not was up to us.

It is not surprising therefore that these normal, ordinary women, as most of us were, behaved in normal, ordinary ways. We did our best to live in ways that we understood. We did not like the circumstances that were imposed upon us and consistently, throughout those three and a half years, we tried to improve conditions, to raise the standards in the Camp, and in this we had a considerable measure of success. Almost all of the women had been asked, often told, to leave Singapore before it fell to the invaders. They chose to stay and to tackle whatever happened. They grumbled, complained, argued and bitched but, throughout, the vast majority remained undefeated. I am convinced it was their ordinariness, their normality, that saw them through.

Dear Philip, although the story of us all, is inevitably my story, seen from my point of view. Who was I?

My parents were nice people, middle class, professional. They were never rich nor poor. My father was benevolent and lovable, my mother acidly critical and amusing. My parents adored animals but were not much concerned with children. My birth was an accident. I was christened Elfrieden and very soon became Freddy for ever more. Once I existed, they devoted themselves wholeheartedly to my welfare. They never had nor thought of having any more children. They indulged me in every possible way and I had to pay a high price for that indulgence. They gave me all they could, in every way, and expected everything in return. Of course, I could not deliver, and I grew up with a sense of failure and guilt.

We lived in New York City. Both my parents were extroverts who loved people and the good things of life. They had a large and varied circle of friends and made more wherever they went, and they went to many places because that was part of the excitement of living. From a very early age, I was part of all their activities and enjoyments. I was also involved in their moods and tempers. They took their pleasures and worries seriously without ever stopping to understand them. I watched, fascinated. I became an observer, a gregarious loner. I grew up in the Twenties and Thirties: Prohibition, the Depression, Noel Coward, Dorothy Parker, Edward Prince of Wales. Hollywood sparkled, Mencken wrote. 'Shrinks' and 'gurus' were unheard of; the wisecrack gave the answer. Wit was the thing.

By the time I was a student, I had already become a rather sophisticated, well-travelled, multi-experienced and pretty cool customer. How then can one explain that, ten years later, as a successful journalist and newspaper executive, I was responsible for a diary that seems to have been written by a young girl in the throes of her first love affair?

A little more autobiography is needed.

I had finished my third year at Barnard College, New York, when, due to my father's worsening heart condition, the family moved to Dublin and I transferred to Trinity College. It was fun and, within eighteen months, I had married a final year medical student who then joined the Indian Medical Service. He was appointed MO of the 5th/14th Punjabi Regiment. I adored India and life was good.

At this point the Fates stepped in and decided to give me a buffeting. They were relentless. I was expecting a much-wanted baby but, in the fifth month, I contracted dysentery and had a nasty miscarriage. War broke out in Europe and the Regiment was sent to Penang. I followed, started another baby, lost it. My father whom I adored, died. He was only fifty-five years old. My husband was twenty-seven and had been an inter-varsity middle-weight boxing champion. Now he developed pleurisy and within a week was dead. All this happened in less than a year. It was too much. I turned myself off emotionally, scared that if I ever let myself love anybody it would mean more tragedy.

I left Penang and went to Singapore where it was easy for me to get a job on the Malaya Tribune Group of Newspapers. Soon afterwards most of the men working there were called up for the Local Defence Corps. I had been writing for magazines and newspapers since I was eleven, when I sold a story to *St Nicholas* magazine to get the money to buy something desirable that my parents thought unsuitable. It was the natural thing for me to write because my mother and father were at home with words and used them easily in speech or on paper. They had always been involved in publishing one thing or another and I was too. As more men on the *Tribune* were called up, so my jobs increased. That was satisfying.

So there I was in Singapore, a 'successful', young, American widow with straight legs and good teeth, and a coat of armour that nobody, but nobody, was going to penetrate. Certainly not that man Philip.

He had been a gynaecologist practising in London and was one of the doctors who, in 1938, had signed a form saying that in case of hostilities he would be prepared to serve full-time. When the war did break out in Europe, he was immediately called up and sent to Singapore as Gynaecological Specialist, Malaya Command. Malaya had many Service families and the need for a 'gynae' man was not as silly as it sounds.

He was then in his mid-thirties (ten years older than I), not bad looking, with a deep, smooth voice and easy, self-assured manner. We had to meet on the social round and I was not too smitten. Most other women found him wildly attractive and that, in itself, was off-putting. I was not going to get involved. This suited him, too, for he had just been through a short disastrous marriage and had decided to 'play the field'.

Later, he told me that he had made up his mind quite early

(11)

on that he was going to marry me when I was again fit for marriage. I doubt whether he ever mentioned his intentions to me but it is unlikely that I would remember, for the idea did not fit in with my attitude and, anyway, I would not have understood what he meant.

We became friends, both feeling secure with each other. We knew that we were both eligible and fair game. In the social climate of Singapore in those days, the game could quickly become a bore. We were not bored with each other and enjoyed the time we spent together. Then on 7/8 December, the Japanese attacked Singapore. Everybody knew it had to happen. The question had been when and where. Now we knew.

It is history that the war in Malaya lasted just seventy days. Much has been written about them. From our point of view, the whole thing was a shambles. Nothing went right. The Japanese army, contrary to expectations, came down the peninsula from the north and our forces did not know how to stop them. Japanese air power knocked out our aerodromes and the few inadequate planes that we had. Singapore was subjected to bombing and shelling. Our big guns were pointed out to the sea and the Japanese offered no targets. They had sunk our *Prince of Wales* and the *Repulse*. We had nothing.

I worked on the paper until it had a direct hit and then donned nurse's uniform to see what I could do at the General Hospital. Philip had been transferred to be in charge of all the Service cases that were taken there.

My nursing qualifications were lamentable. I had only done a St John's First Aid and Home Nursing course in India. My ability to fold many-tailed bandages was excellent but the casualties at the General needed a different approach. Hundreds of sailors, soldiers and civilians, all the victims of bombs, shells, snipers and old-fashioned warfare were brought to the General until the wards overflowed and the corridors were packed. Philip tried to keep track of all the cases. I tried to nurse.

(12)

While all this was building up, everybody tried to induce me to leave. The American Consul advised it, ordered it, and finally washed his hands of me. Philip told me to get out. I could see no sense in going. I had no responsibilities and there was much to be done right there.

Finally Philip got really cross, said that I was unreasonable, that he felt responsible for me and that if he was responsible for me then I had better face the facts and marry him. So there!

Suddenly, I knew that I wanted to marry him, was in love with the guy, wanted to be looked after, no longer be a loner, have someone to love and be loved. I went overboard. I had a reason for living. It was beautiful.

On 6 February, Philip left his work for half an hour, collected me and two friends and, between air raids, we rushed to the Registry Office, got married and returned to the General Hospital. Jewellers were no longer functioning and as a wedding ring we used a cabuchon sapphire ring he had given me some months before.

On 15 February, Singapore fell and one of the first things the Japanese did was to commandeer the General Hospital. Philip had to get all the Service cases out. Makeshift hospitals were set up. One was in the Cricket Club, another in a theatre and the third in Fullerton Building which had been mainly offices but which also housed the Singapore Club. The Club was on two floors with a bar, lounges and a restaurant on one and rooms where members from up-country could stay on the other. The Club atmosphere soon disappeared as hundreds of the more seriously wounded were brought in. Mattresses and 'biscuits' were laid out on the floor of the lounges. The Bursar's and Directors' rooms were turned into operating theatres. In the kitchen, instruments were sterilised, tea brewed and some sort of meals cooked up for patients and worn-out doctors and nurses. Most of the water mains had been hit. There was no pressure and we had to go to the basement and lug up buckets of the precious stuff. The landings were stacked with the bodies of those who had not survived. There was too much to be done and no chance to stop. Rest was not something we took. We worked until sleep overcame us, and then it was back to work again.

At the fall of Singapore, Changi military station had been chosen as the prisoner-of-war camp and gradually all captured Servicemen were sent there. As some of the patients improved they too were sent there and towards the end of the month orders came that Fullerton was to be shut and everybody transferred to Changi. We who were nursing hoped to be allowed to go too, but this was not sanctioned. All the women were told to be ready to be sent to a civilian camp that had been set up in Katong on the outskirts of the city. We were to take food and clothes to last for ten days.

I had gone to Fullerton with a small suitcase containing a few nurse's uniforms and one or two special possessions. Now the facilities of the upper floor of the Singapore Club proved invaluable. They had last been used by up-country wives on their way to escape from Malaya. The last ships that left had been full to overflowing and each passenger had been allowed only a minimum of luggage, so the rooms at Fullerton were full of the clothes that had been jettisoned. The other nurses and I went through them, choosing whatever we thought best for our 'ten-day' stay. The kitchen stores provided a useful assortment of tins.

On 2 March two open lorries came to take us to Katong. We waited outside the building for some time before leaving and during that time Philip and some of the other doctors had the wonderful foresight to collect some mattresses and throw them into the lorries with us. And so, on that hot afternoon, complete with looted clothes, a few tins of food and a mattress, I said goodbye to Philip and started my lonesome honeymoon.

That is where my diary begins.

My darling—This is the first of the letters that should be posted to you—but no luck. Were it possible, this would have been started long ago. As it is, this is the end of our second day here. I'll try to make the report complete; someday you'll read it. You won't be able to read the loneliness then. That is good—we'll be together.

The high official who was to accompany us was detained so we made our way here independently and arrived quite late. At the gates we were searched for cameras, radios or other contraband but we had none, naturally, so that was all right.

We carried our luggage through the first house where I recognised some old friends, local girls mostly who had married soldiers. There were many children and others were obviously on the way. The atmosphere was friendly but not very restful and as we were all dead tired it was good to be told to pass through, past the next house and into the third.

In the gardens there were women working and those with nothing to do helped us with our luggage. The houses are large and the gardens spacious. Odd areas are wired off with suspected land mines. There are papaya trees and some vegetables already sprouting.

The third house—ours—must have been the house of a very large family but it seemed depressingly small to house over one hundred and thirty women (there are over four hundred in the three). We were told that we could have a space four feet by ten each but that was impossible. Ethel [the wife of a very close friend of my first husband. She was a handsome, vibrant Canadian whose past history of nervous disorder was known to me but to nobody else in captivity] and I found room for our beds at the side of some stairs and then went to hunt for the rest of our things. While hunting we found a servants' room outside, next to the latrines—it was empty and, joy of joys, room for only two. So in we moved.

By this time we had found some old (and new) friends and we all cleaned the room, put up the beds and nets and exchanged experiences.

I met Mrs Graham White [wife of the Archdeacon of Singapore] who gave me a warm welcome and a cup of tea. It was grand seeing her again. She gave us every sort of help and showed us around.

The house faces the sea and we may go bathing. There is running water and six latrines which we empty three times a day. The latrine squad changes weekly.

Back to our little go-down—we spent one night there but the 'johnny' atmosphere plus the constant sound of passing feet did not make it ideal. We decided to search further in the morning but to remain if the only alternative was the big house.

Up early and there in a corner of the compound stood an old garage with an oily pit and many chunks of former cars. At one end a rickety staircase led to what had been the syce's [groom/chauffeur] quarters—two small rooms and a verandah. Some of the floor boards had rotted and the sky showed through odd tiles of the roof but we immediately saw its possibilities and were thrilled.

Long before the breakfast bell went our bags and beds were up—carefully balanced on the healthy floor boards. Then began our scrounge for furniture. Before that though, Ethel and I had to decide whom we would allow to share the other half of our mansion. MAS [Medical Auxiliary Service] Mrs Rogers had greeted me with open arms and suggested my joining her crew. Was she worthy of the honour of garaging with us? Not quite. Mrs Graham White (now known as 'Knobs') was adorable but not up to roughing it. Marion [Marion Reyers, the very Hungarian wife of an English businessman and a close friend] was in the house next door. Some people Ethel suggested I didn't like and some I suggested she wouldn't have. Finally we both agreed wholeheartedly on Mrs DeMoubray and the red-headed Clarke [the first, Katherine, the wife of a high official in the Malaysian Civil Service; the second, Kate, a nursing sister.] We met them on the breakfast line and over our cups of tea and bits of bread made our full plans. They were very delighted. While they collected their stuff, Ethel and I went furniture hunting and brought our trophies home—proudly.

Each had found the bottom of a dressing table without a top (two pieces of asbestos did the trick). Ethel's had two doors. Mine had lost one but it was painted a pretty green and later I found what had been the frame of the mirror—most elegant.

10 March 1942

The last few minutes at Fullerton I had picked up a little rattan stool. This gave our cottage class.

Our house had formerly been RAF offices and among the wrecked machines we found two typewriter tops that became bedside tables. Our beds were wonderfully comfortable due to your successful mattress hunt.

Our windows looked out on a Sikh garden but Marion brought us a stout curtain she had picked up in her travels and we soon had complete privacy.

Marion was in the second house sleeping on the floor in a room with eight others. Her reaction to the past few weeks was an irresistible desire to fight with everybody. We did not fight for we did not see very much of each other.

Our crowd of four stuck very much to itself. Ethel became my very good friend and I was delighted to have things organised for me. I was too tired to think or feel. There was a terrific amount of physical work to be done; cleaning and lugging and walking vast distances in search of necessities.

Katherine DeMoubray and I walked to the front house for some wire for the mosquito nets. Ethel and Kate searched elsewhere for nails. We all hunted for a hammer and then climbed the walls on rickety boxes to hammer the nets up.

The second day Knobs came to ask whether we would like to work under her; she was OC Woodchoppers. We were delighted and immediately got busy hoiking lumber, sawing and hacking.

All cooking was done on wood (electricity and gas had been turned off) and a great deal was needed every day. Ethel turned out to be a natural woodchopper (her strength is astounding) but the rest of us were rather clumsy and it was not unexpected when K. DeM sank the axe in her leg. It looked a rotten cut, bled profusely but, she swore, did not hurt. A few days later her injury proved a godsend.

Each house had its own kitchen and cooking staff. Ours was headed by old Miss Medwyn, ex-chorus girl, now a fat sixty-five, who saw that what there was, was on time. The food was inadequate: breakfast tea and a biscuit, lunch rice with watery soup and perhaps a teaspoonful of greens, tea and biscuits at 4.30 and at 7 pm a piece of bread, perhaps buttered or jammed. Thank goodness we had our little private stores, not much but they were something. Every time we had a bite of chocolate or an extra biscuit we'd look at each other and the bites would stick; each wondered whether her husband in Changi was enjoying anything as good.

11 March 1942

We were allowed to go down to the beach, not to stroll or sunbathe, but to swim. This seemed grand and I greatly appreciated the gift of half a yellow bath towel from which to make a swim suit. Every free minute was spent sewing. But there weren't many free minutes. Apart from washing, cleaning, chopping wood, there were the thousand absolutely essential conversations.

As we passed through the gardens we saw Mrs Dickinson, wife of the IGP [Inspector General of Police, who had been badly wounded by a bomb thrown into his office a week before capitulation]. She was planting spinach. Hard to recognise her in a pair of men's khaki shorts, miles too large, and her husband's shirt. She had been allowed to see him twice when he was dangerously ill. Now that he was better she had to wait for news from Dr Hopkins [Eleanor].

Dr H had almost drifted into the job of liaison officer with the JHC [Japanese High Command] and an essential thing it was too, for the lady who was appointed was a horrible failure. Poor Miss E, probably an excellent assistant matron [of one of the hospitals in Malaya], but now completely out of her depth—far more worried about any hidden private tins of Klim [milk powder] than about the inadequacy of our food ration from the JHC. She just had that type of mind. If she could not impress us, how could she impress strangers? When we met Dr H or Miss E we had to stop and ask for news, plans or regulations. Also in the gardens was Mrs Rogers [Bess], still smart though dressed in men's trousers and shirt. Her reactions when I wore my first frock proved that I had looted well. She positively drooled and I was delighted.

Mrs Dive and I relived the last days at General Hospital [Helen, with her doctor husband, had had the room next to ours]. Knobs would chip in little anecdotes, e.g. once just as she was going off to lunch with Graham a Chinese girl asked for a bedpan. Knobs produced it and then went off to food completely forgetting the woman on the pan for almost an hour and a half. Instead of apologetically returning she marched briskly up to the patient, asked, 'Ready?', as if ninety minutes were the usual time, and efficiently removed the pan when the patient proudly nodded assent.

And from bedpans to latrines—at first we had to empty these three times a day in holes dug in the garden. Considering that there were about five hundred women and

children this wasn't a very satisfactory arrangement and after a
few days the Municipality agreed to remove the night soil.
Thus a new problem arose. Six latrines were marked 'Use
these for urine only'. The other six were marked 'Use other
latrines for urine'. If you could only have seen the women
running from one set to the other as they changed their
physical minds. Incidentally almost everybody suffered from
constipation.

Mrs Moir [Nelly, wife of Brigadier Bobby Moir] was in
House Two with Lady Heath [Katherine, wife of Lieutenant-
General Sir Lewis M. Heath] and five others. She did not
seem too happy and often visited us in what had become
known as Woodchoppers' Cottage. Many people dropped in
for a chat and a bit of privacy. We were beautifully settled and
very happy when orders came through that we were being
moved to Changi jail. Some of our luggage would be driven
out; we would have to walk [fourteen kilometres]. It was a
blow. Beach House was pretty awful but we had cleaned it and
settled in, the gardens were doing well, there was the sea,
plenty of water in the taps. Now Changi jail.

14 March 1942

Darling, I must somehow catch up with this darned diary and
so to blazes with details of the last days in our beloved
Woodchoppers' Cottage. I'll just mention the wonderful
meals, as we hogged tins we knew we could not pack. We
stored energy for the long walk and one girl even unearthed a
bottle of sherry with which to swill down asparagus tips and
sardines. Most of us packed convinced that we would never
see half our things again and our few possessions had become
so precious. And here I must take off my hat to absolutely
every one of the women; they just would not let it get them
down. They were darned annoyed but not one would let

herself get too depressed. Under the most unpleasant circumstances they could be heard laughing and teasing each other.

On Sunday 8 March we lugged all our baggage to the front gate and then formed up in lines of five. If only you could have seen us — the very old or ill were driven but the rest covered a great span of years, types and temperaments. We had all dressed with only one idea, comfort. Style had gone west. We wanted protection from the sun and the greatest care for our feet.

I looked splendid in my khaki trousers and the looted white evening blouse which was the only thing I owned with long sleeves. On my head was a nurse's veil tied like a turban, with the brim of a looted hat (I had cut out the low crown) on top to keep out the sun. Flung over my back in a haversack arrangement was the little bright blue bag (we had been told not to expect our luggage for two or three days) and a bottle of water, and to finish the ensemble was the big black looted umbrella to be used either as a walking stick or sun shade.

Can you imagine five hundred women dressed in similar haphazard fashion marching forth under a strong, armed guard?

In the very first line stood Ethel, Kate, Marion, Mrs Moir and me. Katherine, having hacked her leg, was allowed to ride which suited us down to the ground. She was going to prepare tea for our arrival and also book rooms for us.

We had been told that we were to be put in the European cells, that these were not too bad at all, each with its own johnny [lavatory], wee bedroom and sitting room. Three of us were to share one of these flatlets. Still cramped but not too bad.

The walk was long and uneventful. It was not as bad as I had expected. When one saw people like Mrs Dickinson and Mrs Dive trudging along [who were twenty or thirty years older than I was], I felt so glad of my long, healthy young

(2 1)

limbs that even fatigue was ruled out. The haversack became darned heavy but luckily after five or six miles a lorry with Dr Hopkins passed by slowly and I flung it on her lap.

The Japanese soldiers who formed our guard were unexpectedly kind, allowed us to stop every mile or even less, helped us get water and even tried to rig up foot gear for those whose shoes had got the best of them.

The people on the streets paid little attention to us. We were neither cheered nor jeered which was really rather surprising considering what an odd parade we made.

The last mile was long and I imagined what it must have been like for those who walked from Fullerton Building [two miles from Beach House] and then had two more miles to go [to the Military Camp]. Men or not — feet are feet.

A number of women fell out and had to be picked up but the vast majority struggled on and as we came in sight of the prison we all got into step, and singing at the top of our voices, we marched through the high walls. The men at the other side cheered themselves hoarse. We felt as if we really had done something.

16 March 1942

The prison is not a very happy-looking place. Nothing but grey walls and bars. Not a single tree or shrub. Hardly a blade of grass.

Katherine greeted us with rolls she had picked up on the way and a tin of sardines. I don't remember anything ever tasting so good. While we munched she told us the awful state of affairs.

There had been absolutely no preparation made for our arrival. There was one big room in which fifty people could lie down, if they had no luggage and were willing to lie skin to skin. Otherwise nothing. What luggage of ours had arrived she had dragged into a corner of a corridor and now we would have to wait and see.

I just didn't care. My mattress was there and in no time I was three-quarters asleep. My getting worried and running about looking was not going to help things any.

After perhaps an hour word came round that a new wing had been opened and that we should choose our cells. Up we went—to the Chinese part of the prison—rows and rows of nine-by-twelve-foot cells with great concrete slabs on which to sleep and Chinese lavatories [slits in the floor, known as 'squatters'] (dirty) in the corner. The walls were high, bleak and filthy, and up about ten feet were little windows. We could have a cell each. There was privacy but, my God, it was hell.

For the first time I felt an incontrollable anger surge up in me. For almost thirty years I had tried to develop into something that would be worthy of a love like yours. That something could not, would not, be stuck in a disease-infected, inhuman cell. Not for a day, nor for an hour—and here was the prospect of years. They could do what they wished with me but they would have to lock and tie me in before I'd stay in those cells.

Some of the women did not seem to mind so much, which was good, for most of them are still living in those holes of concrete. We waited while they moved in and then went off searching. Luckily we found a helpful officer who took us around, and down on the ground level at the end of what had been the recreation room we found a tool-room, fairly large, full of implements, instruments and shelves. He said that if we took care of the stores we might stay in the tool-room. Feeling much better we moved in—Katherine (DeM), Kate, Ethel, Mrs Moir and me. And there at the moment of writing we still are.

Now we love our tool-room with the same passion as we had for Woodchoppers' Cottage. Our five beds are put up about three feet apart. The others all had table-cloths or regular bedspreads with which to cover theirs, and I felt rather left out until I remembered the heavy green canvas that had been our impromptu bed rolls. By splitting one length and sewing the halves on either side of the whole with thick green wool I made a really fine spread. The green cushions that were to be my bed before you copped the mattresses, blend beautifully. Next to my bed are my three shelves. The bottom one holds a few books, sewing materials, soap and toothbrush, etc. The second shelf is the important one, for besides comb, brush, eau de cologne, it holds your picture (and Mother's).

You know, Philip, I never liked that photograph at all but now it's become the most understanding thing in my small world. When I'm happy you smile. When I'm worried your picture regrets that it hasn't a shoulder for me to cry on. Sometimes when I stare at it very hard wondering whether you are taking care of yourself (we are told there are one hundred new cases of dysentery at Changi every day), whether circumstances are not too terrible for you, your picture seems to wink.

19 March 1942

Before I tell you more about this amazing Camp I must mention Judy. When we were waiting outside Fullerton Building to be escorted to Beach House, a little fox terrier who had visited the hospital once or twice came to play with us. We waited a long time and when we eventually left we lifted the pup into the lorry with us.

To our amazement many of the women had brought their dogs into internment with them. There were beautiful setters, sheepdogs, spaniels, pekinese, so our little fox terrier caused little attention. Judy became part of Woodchoppers' Cottage and slept under my bed. When word came through that we were to move to Changi, orders were given that the dogs would have to be left behind. The last night some of the women dosed their pets with veronal. The men were going to shoot the rest after we left. What to do with Judy? She did not belong to anyone in particular, so no one in particular was responsible for putting her in the cage with the other dogs. We just ignored her hoping that some Chinese family would feed and take care of her. She is a very well-bred, attractive dog. But Judy had her own ideas— she just trotted beside us all the way to Changi and when we walked into the jail, she walked with us. No one said a word and now Judy lives with us in our tool-room. During the day she goes around visiting and makes women happy by letting them play with her. At meal times and at night she comes back to us. She sleeps on one of my green cushions, eats out of the top of a thermos (mine broke on the way to Beach House). We think she is expecting puppies; another week should tell. The other day the storekeeper found a tin of Lactol biscuits which we are keeping in case of the blessed event.

The Lactol are a difficulty because we are all generally so hungry that we want to eat them ourselves. So far the tin remains closed. But it was touch and go the other day when Lady Heath came in complaining bitterly of the lack of food; she is expecting a baby and we felt she really needed something. Suddenly the humour of the situation struck us. Pregnant Lady Heath visiting us in the tool-room of the jail and we showing our hospitality by 'almost' offering her dog biscuits.

By the way, on the last page I mentioned the 'men' shooting the dogs. These men were four who were left behind to do difficult manual labour for us. They carried the sacks of rice, put up shelves, built latrines.

From the dog biscuits to the food at Changi—the first three days there was practically nothing except tea and rice. Many were hungry. Luckily I seemed to have a smaller appetite than most for, though I was dissatisfied, I was not hungry. This might have been due to the watery tummy that just would not leave and it might have been due to the fact that I had firmly made up my mind that nothing about this internment was going to get me down if humanly possible. I had stayed because I wanted to be with you and because I did not believe in running away. I was fully aware what the consequences might be and had expected them to be worse. What's the good of grousing? No matter how long this internment is, it must be temporary. Some day we'll get together and, regardless of what sort of mess this world is in, I firmly believe that we have found something that will remain fine and untouched.

I am going to try to stay as healthy as possible, to learn odd things that might be useful (not knitting!) and to keep away from all the squabbling. If there is work to be done, I'll gladly do it. So far there has been none that is really interesting. I stand behind the counters and serve food and have learned all sorts of funny things about the women from that. I clean up my bits and pieces, wash my clothes, play with Judy, chat, sleep, read (not much) and plan (incessantly) how we might get together.

You were not meant to be a prisoner-of-war. Your mind, your attitude, your body are all wrong for jail. You are a great doctor and a greater man. You must not be wasted and so I plan and plan and plan and talk to your photograph.

20 March 1942

Today had a mild physical examination by one of the Camp doctors (Cicely Williams) who is doing everyone in an effort to see how the peculiar diet affects us. She expects the worst saying that we are getting one quarter of what we are used to and one half of what we need (this statement was made the first week of Camp—food has improved some since then). She was surprised at my excellent condition (yippee). I wasn't—sleep, eat, continuously; any time seems good for a rest and any food regardless of taste is stuffed down. If only I knew that you are taking similarly good care of yourself.

There are many lorries all along the road (they can be seen from some of the higher floors) and we are wondering whether you men will be moved from the Military Camp. We get no real news from outside. Since 13 March the *Syonan Times* [an English-language newspaper put out by the Japanese] appears more or less regularly. On that day final victory over the NEI [Netherlands East Indies] was announced. But apart from big events of that sort the paper says little and as at General Hospital a million and one rumours are rife. Cutting all our communications cannot stop them. The last few days we have been hearing many loud explosions; they might be bombers or they might be naval guns. Each possibility becomes some woman's conviction—and will she part with it? N.b.l.!

Then of course there are the varying interpretations of the *Times*. A statement cannot mean what it says it must mean ...

I accept what pleases me but believe nothing. Honest! Often think of your repeated remarks re my gullibility. Think of all your statements and smile. What a ludicrous combination we must have been. You saying truths over and over and I grimly saying, 'Undoubtedly' but feeling nothing.

21 March 1942

These days the Camp (we refuse to call it prison) is a seething mass of politics. Conversational bubbles of upheaval go pop wherever one looks. There is to be a grand election of officers to hold office for all of six months.

At Beach House where there were three separate buildings politics were fairly simple. Each house had a house representative whose activities were necessarily curtailed by the hectic conditions (anyway we in our little syce's quarters never felt their influence). There was also the head Camp representative, a poor, stammering, ineffectual, ex-assistant matron who got her post because she happened to be born while her parents were travelling through now neutral Spain. The important people were the Camp shoppers, (ours was Mrs Nelson [Kathleen], now in Myako, the old Mental Hospital—suspected appendix) who could go out into the wide world and buy things.

22 March 1942

(Interruption: Katherine and Ethel brought in a whole coconut—don't know where they cadged it and we had a fine time finishing it. Today Kate has collywobbles.)

To get back to elections. When we arrived here, a temporary committee was got up, Dr Hopkins as head. We got Katherine DeMoubray in as our floor member. And everything seemed to be going as smoothly as could be expected. Of course there was a certain amount of bickering and dissatisfaction to be heard; that's the worst of a democracy, one can hear the discontent.

(Goodness gracious, will I never be able to get on with this report? At this point yesterday, my bed broke and I had to spend the rest of the afternoon mending it. Found a length of canvas hose-pipe, split it, cut it into straps and nailed it all up and bed is now as good as new. My, how nice it will be to sit on a regular chair again. Have not seen one in the entire place.)

Let's cut the politics short. Dr Hopkins was the only one put up for liaison officer and was consequently re-elected. Both Ethel and Katherine were nominated for deputies but a Mrs Gregory Jones [Hilary] got in. Now nominations are open for

House Head (the other two deal directly with the Nipponese—this one is to look after our own personal troubles, e.g. drains, dirty floors, disposal of rubbish and lights out). So many have been nominated that there is bound to be discontent about whoever is chosen. It's a thankless job and one of its main problems is the treatment of our large Eurasian population. Some of these Eurasians are charming but the majority are not and say they are married to British soldiers (some with no more proof than a couple of half-white children). One woman has not seen her husband for five years yet claims the protection of this Camp. I am surprised at the Nipponese allowing them to stay, for it is such an obvious ramp. Here they get better food, quarters and care than they have ever had and all for nothing. The better food applies at least to those with children, for they (we have almost sixty children from tiny infants up to nine years old) get all the extras that are ever brought in—fruit, buns, etc.—today they had eggs. The Eurasians with children were put into the few European cells, as they were roomier and had running water. In the short time we are here they have made them incredibly dirty. Cleaning squads can do little as the women refuse to move even temporarily during cleaning.

Yesterday there was a free-for-all fight and one woman landed in hospital. Also Dr Hopkins discovered some of the children playing football with buns they had tasted and not liked. In the meantime many of the pregnant mothers (there are ten) are almost crying with hunger. It is a very difficult situation and I am afraid none of us is big enough to solve it.

24 March 1942

(Did I ever mention that we have bedbugs? Very distressing!)

Return to politics (just slightly). I was asked if I would be willing to be put up for some of the offices, but refused. Will do my share of the dirtiest work but otherwise want peace. There is no personality here so outstanding that she can influence the entire Camp and the garrison. The state of this place depends on the Nipponese and the women themselves en masse. My sacrificing my not-very-effectual self for the 'cause' would have little influence on the whole. And there are so many things I enjoy doing: have sewn and carpentered a bit and have about four short stories ready to be typed—yesterday spent almost an hour sketching. It was fun. Also thoroughly enjoy serving the food—one can change the women's expressions so easily. Somehow making them (each one) believe that she is getting a larger sardine or a bit more gravy seems to change the very taste of the food they are eating.

From tomorrow on am doing four hours a day in the hospital. Must get up to be on duty at eight every other day—it's a bit early. The hospital is a bit of a farce but greatly improved in the past week. Now everyone sleeps on beds and there are two chamber-pots and a couple of thermometers. Will be able to tell you more after I've been on a while. Most of the patients are just senile cases, the rest 'dysentery'. No one's bowels are in order—can't be on this unusual rice diet—some have diarrhoea (Kate dictated spelling of same) and others are constipated. If the diarrhoea gets you down it's called dysentery and you go to hospital. Kate was on duty today and came back very pleased with life; she gave a woman an enema and out came a tapeworm.

Miss Stewart, who became matron at General when Miss Braemore left, is in hospital with a liver. Went to visit her yesterday and she told me that in the pockets of the car in which she was driven to internment was a photo of me (playing with dog in garden). Must have been your car. Gee, will have to save to buy another.

Returning to the blooming politics, wonder whether you are being governed according to your old ranks or whether you too have elections? (See Lady Heath quite often—knew her before her marriage—and have heard many interesting sidelights on this war; hope I remember them—just for fun! She, incidentally, is very anxious to see whether she could not get you to attend her at her confinement—probably June.)

27 March 1942

Oh, darling, what a lot has piled up since, the last entry. Starting with the least important, my hospital work. There is little nursing to do so I make beds, sweep and wash patients. Some of the very old ladies are a bit batty and most amusing. Those that can walk like me very much for I have introduced a new way of washing them; take them into the bathroom, soap them all over (quite an experience, so many of their bits and pieces are draped and hardly available), then stand them over our difficult, flat, Asiatic johnnies and sloosh warm water over them. They giggle like school girls (one of them had her seventy-second birthday today). Matron was a bit horrified at first but now approves.

For two days I fed a sick baby. Today I had to measure it for its coffin—one of the grimmest experiences of my life.

The major happening next to be recorded is the ruination of our tool-shed. Due to the machinations of some most unpleasant old women all the tools were removed—they wanted to move in with us. When it was discovered that they needed commodes and special care they were transferred to hospital but our room was emptied and now five other damsels have been moved in. Of course that spoils everything and we haven't room to turn round. I don't care because I still won't let anything whatsoever (except the cells) get me down but the rest are in a morbid state.

It came at a most inopportune moment, for the nerves of two of our five had become very frayed. Kate has had hysterics more than once and is in an almost suicidal state. It is amazing but those who have had happiness before feel they will regain it. While those who never had it feel that now all hope is lost.

Nellie Moir too feels that she cannot stand much more. Katherine varies but is so busy trying to run this and that (fairly successfully) that she usually forgets to inquire how she is reacting. Ethel has been splendid and I, my dear, have you.

28 March 1942

And now to the burning issue: three days ago a notice was posted on the board saying that the JHC asks for names of volunteers to run a canteen at the Sea View Hotel. Names to be in at 6 p.m.

Some immediately said that any form of work (except nursing) for the enemy was showing disloyalty to one's country. Others said, 'Thank God! A chance to get out of this hell hole. Another month of this and we shall be mad or dead.' Many said, 'Under certain conditions—in the interests of international goodwill—perhaps it will make them treat our own people kinder—' All said, 'What's behind it?' And the discussions were endless.

Lady Heath felt that if women just went out willy nilly, some (we are a very mixed crowd) would disgrace us and possibly start unnecessary incidents. She was willing to send a list of questions to the JHC and if the answers were satisfactory she would be willing to be responsible for a group of women vetted by her. She would also want her husband's approval. All the Military wives agreed.

All this had to go through the Committee and these ladies have so far been too busy with all the other business on hand to do anything about it. Besides, they don't quite know what to do for it is a great responsibility and the Committee, though

(32)

composed of fine women, is unaccustomed to its work. We do not know conditions outside nor do we know the Japanese mentality.

The night the notice was posted the list of names was demanded. The Chairman replied that the list could not be handed over until the questions were answered. That was impossible so an impasse was reached and the matters still stand.

Except for nursing I would not go out unless as a member of a military unit under the leadership of either Lady Heath or Mrs Moir. Unless, of course, it becomes a general thing—but I think even then. In spite of this decision I feel that the offer might very easily have been a goodwill attempt on the part of our captors.

When we get out people will ask how we have been treated and we will have to tell that we were first crowded in three inadequate houses, then walked miles to a jail where we had to double up in filthy cells of Chinese convicts. As civilian internees and especially as nursing sisters this was not fair treatment.

My own personal contacts have been different and have proved my former conviction that most individuals no matter where or when are human beings.

A guard came in one day while men were carting wood through our room (there is a through passage from the hall to the double walls). I had been resting and slipped on my navy blue kimono. The guard looked at me and suddenly his face lit up. He came and like an incredulous little boy asked, 'Japanese?' I nodded and then he most politely showed me how to wrap the kimono, what length it should be and how the obi should be worn. It was like a Scot finding a kilt in Tokyo.

Another guard who had to spend a whole afternoon in the tool-shed while men collected tools, helped us fold our washing, then asked Ethel for a coloured hankie and finally requested a few drops of perfume for it. When he had what he wanted he daintily tucked it away and looked most happy.

During another long visit one soldier very carefully inspected everything on my shelf. Smelt each bottle, asked how the nail stuff was used and wanted to know whether you were my father or husband and expressed regret that you were at the Military Camp and not here where I could see you.

Today a soldier brought some flowers, wild but beautifully arranged, to the hospital.

All of which is very difficult.

30 March 1942

Ah, never a dull moment! During inspection by a high officer yesterday, Buckley (sister who was so unhappy in Fullerton Building) refused to stand up and asked, 'Why should I?' Result—she has been confined to her room for three days and everything has been considerably tightened for us. A few men have been biffed and the odd woman prodded. You should see us bow and stand to attention now. I feel quite hurt when the sentries look the other way and don't see me going through my act.

Last night Dr Hopkins and Dr Williams came and asked whether I would edit a camp newspaper. Am quite tickled with the idea. We cannot use the jail printing press and we have very little paper, so the first edition which will, I hope, come out on Wednesday will be type-written—one to each block. Tentative name: *The Changi Pow-Wow*. Have already received a number of contributions. Will report further developments.

Today the High Command came around and asked whether the nursing sisters would be willing to go out and work. Answer seems to be, 'Not unless as a unit and a guarantee that it won't be another false alarm.'

Ethel has been trying to get a Red Cross canteen but so far in vain. Today she is in the throes of work much like Fullerton for she has started what at home we would call an Elephant Party, 'Bring something, Buy something—proceeds to the Red Cross.' I gave some unnecessary powder puffs and bought a green Aertex blouse. Thank goodness for my two pairs of gum-soled shoes. A pair someone had contributed had to be auctioned and went for over $30. Wonder how you are managing? Do wish you had taken more with you. You're so frightfully impractical about yourself. Wonder whether any of the batmen I hired for you materialised?

2 April 1942

Lots of bits and pieces in the last two days. Didn't feel too well on Tuesday and at lunchtime, while bending over the big wooden tub serving rice, suddenly felt myself melting into it, while each kernel went pop with a splash of black and yellow lights. Later, while lying down, made the depressing but not surprising discovery that I was not expectant. Anyway, did no work that day and had to go hard at it to get the paper *Weekly Pow-Wow* out by noon yesterday. Typed ten copies, four pages each, and the reception has been surprisingly good. Do enjoy the work so much more than committee nonsense.

Lady Heath went shopping for layettes for the pregnant mothers and brought us Military wives the odd present (chocolate ginger for me—now ain't I glad you're a Major?). (Honey, I love you very much—sometimes it just drowns me in big sweeping waves.)

Since a couple of days ago the men have taken over all the cooking and the rationing is much, much better. Buns every other day and porridge for breakfast twice a week. No fresh meat yet but the other day we got five sardines each and the bully beef ration has risen to a quarter of a tin per person.

Which is all quite sufficient. Fresh vegetables have been promised. Looking back now at the days when we got six tins of soup to feed two hundred and eighty-five women, can't imagine how the kitchen staff managed. Could kick self six times around this jail for giving you such a tiny orange cup instead of a good-sized mug. Did you manage to swop?

Incidentally just realised that I never explained who 'the men' are. You probably know—the jail is very large and all civilian men were interned here before our arrival. They just opened some extra wings. Now special fatigues of men come over to lug wood or build shelters, benches, etc. for us. They also bring the meals three times a day. Have not seen anyone we both know. The men who come are always those with wives in Camp. Some of the guards are charming and let husbands and wives chat or share a cup of tea. Others are bullies and show off their power whenever they can.

It makes one's heart bleed to see some of the older men hoiking heavy planks while anxious-eyed wives walk alongside trying to look unconnected yet pouring out their hearts in fragments of conversation. And we all pass dried prunes, bits of coconut, cigarettes or soap across to them and get more thanks and gallant compliments than we ever heard before. There may be certain weaknesses and squabbles but beneath them there lies an unselfish unity that is noble and fine. There have been many times since we are here that I have been genuinely proud to be a human being.

It was good last night, standing in the top yard of the jail where the only grass grows, watching a perfect double rainbow. You must have seen it too for we both seemed to meet in its beauty. Again I know that this separation, these walls and all that's in and out of them, are a blasted nuisance but nothing more. A waste and an inconvenience but we are so much bigger, so far beyond its effects.

(Later—same day, horribly proud—you'd hate it—gave one of the men a copy of our paper. He showed it to General

Mr Rae who was so impressed that he is having copies made and distributed to all. Often disliked your criticism but now miss it, miss it, miss it.

It's a month today since we left Fullerton Building. If we are incarcerated for a year, then one twelfth is done. If for two years, then a twenty-fourth. Seems easier to swallow in small portions.)

This letter has become a great solace. Can't help feeling that once a thing is written here you automatically read it. Must force self not to write messages to Denis, DeMoubray or Moir, from their wives.

Do hope that you are writing a letter too—then someday when we are in our home we'll curl up on a sofa in front of the fire and you read mine and I'll read yours.

Apropos nice: one nice thing about having lost everything is that now we'll be able to give each other so many presents. 'Sluvly!

4 April 1942

Many little things have happened since last entry so here's a series of flashes. Thursday evening long conversation with Lady Heath. She is charming, tactless, unafraid, clever but does not always look before she jumps. Find it a good idea to make her formulate her thoughts before going into action and to judge from the way she is pawing the ground she is ready for a gallop at any minute. In many ways she reminds me of Ethel, who is energetically unwinding the Red Cross into masses of red tape in which she already is badly entangled; some are suggesting a hanging.

I carry on in solitary reserved state. Have in over a month had regular conversations with only three people; Katherine DeMoubray, Katherine Heath and Marion. Have no desire to increase the number. Am obsessed with two ideas: i) that you and I be let out to finish your work on maternity in one of the local hospitals, ii) that the internees be transferred to Cameron Highlands with a six months' supply of staples and the opportunity to grow whatever else they need. There is constant difficulty now in transporting food and I do not see that it would be much more difficult up there. No one else agrees. It would be so much better for all. Here we are an embarrassing problem for the Japanese. As time goes on we will be even more so. Some have gone decidedly queer already and the sentries too are getting bored; one slapped a passing woman really hard yesterday—there was no reason and many witnesses. Unnecessary incident.

Later—sometimes the gorgeous laziness of this place flows over one like warm oil. Am lying in bed, warmly toasted from this morning's sun, full of enough quite edible food, have just finished an enjoyable book and two chocolates. If I can just imagine that you'll be home for tea, life would be almost too much. Fie, fie for being such a carnal wretch.

Incidentally, after watching a score of women cavorting naked and unashamed under the communal showers (we bathe in the privacy of a back alley and two buckets), have come to a conclusion: that for women to be completely immodest among themselves is a sign of imperfect sex life. No woman whose body is appreciated by a man could display it so easily among so utterly unappreciative an audience as a group of women.

Flash: our bedbugs are becoming a real nuisance and one of the medicos has ordered a general fumigation. We are not looking forward to it and wonder slightly where we will sleep while it is being done. I would sooner drape myself over the high wall than try a cell, even temporarily.

Had intended to leave personalities and gossip, slander, etc. out of this letter but it is becoming almost impossible, for they play such a part in one's life. Main feud is between Ethel (the flamboyant Colonial) and her Red Cross people, versus Dr Hopkins, Bess Rogers and the MAS St John's crowd. Am not taking sides (though am naturally lumped with Ethel—flamboyant American) but am disgusted that the natural and inevitable leaders of this Camp should have to squabble. Am especially disappointed in Dr Hopkins who is working very hard as Camp Representative but whose manner utterly discourages anyone from co-operating with or working under her.

All the fuss, bother and backbiting now going on about the Easter arrangements.

6 April 1942

Cannot remember an Easter since childhood with so much atmosphere and celebration. It started with a sunrise service in the upper *padang*. Oh, Philip, I do hope you see the dawn—in the west the moon like a hole in the dark sky and in the east a delicate sun rising under the careful vigilance of a bright morning star. Slowly the black bulk of the prison lightens until it glimmers and glows like a pink opal. And in the middle of this beauty a handful of women lifting their feeble voices to their Lord, rejoicing that He had arisen, asking for His protection, liberation and the return of their furniture, linen and clothes. The one thing that makes me feel completely outside and apart from the Camp is the escape to religion that all the females are seeking. It's not deep yet it seems to satisfy them. Yesterday at the sunrise service the utter pathos of the scene grabbed me and shook me with uncontrollable sobs. Darling, one can feel so sorry for humanity.

There were many other services throughout the day—RC, C of E, Salvation Army. Little presents were exchanged. Best frocks were worn. The Japanese sent in flowers. Ethel played whirlwind and arranged a sitdown supper under auspices of the Red Cross. The tables looked most civilised but the work involved was terrific. Lady H had the weeps and almost couldn't attend. Had to talk her into it. She is not popular and her actions are carefully watched and criticised. Nelly Moir has become her lady-in-waiting or handmaiden and vacillates between servile devotion and petulant irritation.

9 April 1942

Easter ended with an impromptu party of our crowd. A tin was opened (mushroom soup) and poured over the rice. Jokes popped up and for no reason we had a grand time, ending up picking bedbugs off the mosquito nets.

The first two days of the week were depressing—chuckful of rumours, most fantastic and all without foundation. A guard told us that Berlin had fallen. Another swore that sixteen hundred of us would be sent to Africa within a week. There was more talk of St Johns Island and some or all of us being let out on parole. One can take all the talk with many grains of salt but they do affect one. Then Ethel has gone quite haywire with her Red Cross. The usual fantastic energy with absolutely no system. She has won the adoration of a certain crowd but antagonised Dr Hopkins and the Committee. For some time I had to share their prejudice being considered a passive partner of Mulvany and Co. By dint of diplomacy have managed to steer a course between the two. A terrific reception of the newspaper was probably responsible. On Monday had a fine, helluva row with Bess Rogers. Won the first round and am now letting others carry on the feud for me. After annoying days, lie in bed and check up on the happenings of the day to see which were worth spoiling a day for. Usually find I've been a sucker and that it hasn't been worth it. On the whole think this Internment Camp is darned funny. At first missed a real friend terribly. At every corner queue or situation there was a gap where Ruth should have

(40)

heen [Ruth Swann, a friend who died on the day of the fall of Singapore], but now slowly Katherine DeMoubray is taking her place. Every evening after lights out we sit out in the alley and smoke a last cigarette (running very short!) and discuss past, present and future. Marion too is a good sort but so foreign that real intimacy is impossible, for there cannot be perfect understanding.

12 April 1942

Have a thousand things to do but feel like writing, so—Our lives the past few days continue much as they would in a girls' school, cliques, friendships, feuds, etc. Much excitement when $2000 worth of stuff arrived from Gian Singh [an Indian general store in Singapore]. I bought a half share in a mug with Katherine. Of course there were not enough things for everyone to buy what she wanted and dreadful rows took place. Still are. Shoes are the biggest problem but seem unprocurable. Some are already going barefoot. News came through that the *Karu* which sailed on 13 February was bombed—quite a few casualties. Julius Fisher drowned. Bisseker and John Bagnal saved [three Singapore businessmen]. Didn't know any of the nursing sisters named as saved or lost. Very persistent rumour too that we will be shipped to Portuguese East Africa. Can't see it happening as there is said to be a fourteen to one ration in favour of the conquerors and I doubt whether militaristically one of us women is worth fourteen Japanese men. However it's not far from Lourenço Marques to Durban [where Philip's family lived] and it's a thought to be played with. In the meantime we are fighting persistently for communications with Changi Military. It's hopeful. This morning news came through that Colombo had fallen. Mebbe. Last night a very charming middle-aged woman (Mrs Woodhouse) died and we all feel rotten about that. This afternoon news came through that Mrs Hannay died in Myako. Yesterday two men died. It really is an appalling mortality rate and is not likely to decrease. Please God the Military Camp is well run and you are taking care of yourself. In spite of the many deaths and the lack of comfort the morale of the Camp remains magnificent—though the manners are appalling. Personally prefer a mob of squabbling, selfish females to a Camp of depressed wailing ladies. Often wonder how the outside world will react to us when we are let loose. We will be so hardened to certain things and so naively thrilled with others. With all this talk of exchange to Lourenço Marques thought how doggone funny it would be if I presented myself with your letter to your family and then with a sweeping gesture said, 'And these are my friends,' pointing to the crocodile that walked from Katong to Changi. Katherine says she has cousins in Durban and could take half with her.

We went out on a rampage on Friday night. We had been to a general knowledge test (I hoping to get howlers for *Pow-Wow*). It turned out to be a schoolgirl entertainment and bored us stiff. At the end we climbed to the top floor and up on some boxes and had a look, through the grille, at your Changi and the sea and the whole world. Then we paid a number of calls and finally found a room, uninhabited, with some shelves that led to high windows from which we could get another view. Up we climbed. Judy, who still hasn't had her pups, stayed behind barking her disapproval of our simian activities. The neighbours watched our progress and *joie de vivre* with silent disapproval. We enjoyed ourselves. Then called on K. Heath who was having her fortune told so we had to clear out. Continuing our rampage Bess Rogers came up and handed me a pipe of peace. Most unexpected but gratifying, for I am *not* going to fight with anyone—regardless. The evening ended with us chewing dog biscuits in bed. We think ourselves (K and I) no end civilised and above the horde. Golly!

Well, the paper's out again and can sit down for a quiet chat with you. Quiet is not the right word, for never in my life have I thought it possible to live in such an infernal din. Just imagine the small confines of these prison walls, the echo, the acoustics. Most of the communal activities take place in the big hall just outside our room. The wall goes up for only eight feet and then continues as wire mesh. Just now the dancing class is carrying on to the strains of the *Merry Widow Waltz* on a cracked record. Children are playing because it is raining. The food queues are lining up and there is the clank of dishes. Two women are trying to build a chair and there is the hammering. And of course there is the constant chatter, chatter, chatter. I can sleep through it but it took a long time. The gramophone is the joy of our lives. Never knew how much music meant to me, especially music that suggests bodies in action. The first time Judy Good (new inmate here, not the dog) took out her records, I danced for a solid hour — out in the courtyard all by myself. It truly satisfied a need. How good it will be when we can dance together again and go to ballets and other recitals. Oh, how many things there are that we must do.

Sometimes get so irrationally frightened that anything might happen to either of us and we will be cheated of all that our love promised. Look after yourself, please look after yourself.

18 April 1942

Many pleasant little interludes in the past days. Had my fortune told (everybody does — proceeds to the Red Cross) and was told the very nicest things — we'll get together surprisingly soon, have a very happy home and a son and a daughter. Bilge maybe—but did enjoy hearing it. Next was that the atmosphere in the room has cleared considerably. Ethel was 'sent to Coventry' as she transferred all her energy from the room to her Red Cross shop. Nothing we had was safe, everything was indiscriminately handed out and various fibs followed. 'Twas most unpleasant and I was very worried again but things have much improved. Next had a few diarrhoea-less days for first time. It hadn't been very bad but inconvenient and I have dropped to less than nine stone. Felt grand otherwise and normal tummy just made it perfect. Next—talk that repatriation was getting on—imagined a shipload of badly-wounded plus some doctors (that meant you) leaving here—I would be able to contact Mother—and then you and I would be able to meet perhaps in your Dad's home—Mmmm. Next: Victor Hitch, the chemist from Taiping, sent me some cigarettes and sweets. Hadn't even seen him here and thought it most decent (we ran out of cigarettes about a week ago). Will now undertake his mending. One does feel envious when the husbands on fatigue see their wives and you are so infernally far away. Furthermore stuff came in from Gian Singh—cloth, sand-shoes, odds and ends and food. Surprise ration of bread and an egg for breakfast. We had fresh meat on Wednesday. Often wonder how you react to this dog food. Gosh, it will be fun making special dishes when we get out. Very funny here—just when we are told that rations are so short that we will soon starve, special rations arrive. As soon as starvation and malnutrition are mentioned I feel very weak and wan, no matter how full of food I am. Oh, just remembered we have a dramatic Russian woman here. One day when rumours of Russian successes were going strong we had paste and honey (paste: corn flour and water). She looked at her ration and moaned, 'My country does zo well and zis is all the (excuse pliz) honey I get?' Me, I love her—she's the one who told the fortunes.

(44)

Am fed up with this war. There's been quite enough. Those who wanted to make money or get killed or decorated have had the opportunity. I've had enough jail, enough being parted from you, enough jail. If it had to be, it's all been very interesting but, as mentioned before—enough. And so to bed.

24 April 1942

Oh, darling, the utter luxury of quiet—am in hospital with something like mild dengue [a tropical fever]—backache, headache, mild fever and feel bloody (no longer too bloody, this third day of bed). Was rolled over here yesterday. Kate and Katherine got the wheelchair and we started off along the various corridors and courtyards. They were not too expert and landed me first in a sentry and then in a lorryload of vegetables. Rolled into bed weak with laughter and the trip and they put up the mosquito net and lo and behold—had brought my own bed bugs. More delight. In the afternoon excitement because the JHC personally interviewed all unmarried women under forty. Object seemed to be to see which would be suitable for outside work. No one knows. Marion's planchette says we'll be out in a fortnight but it also says that Arthur is dead, probably by drowning. Planchette as reliable as other rumours. Lady Thomas [wife of Sir Shenton Thomas, the Governor of Singapore] back to fold day before yesterday [she had been in hospital]. St George's Day yesterday, also a celebration. Boiled ham, an egg, etc. our festive rations. I would be in hospital sipping Marmite. Oh, couple of days ago Katherine Heath got out and saw her husband. In the surprise she quite forgot to ask and tell all the things she had planned. He is said to have looked awful and

(45)

reported thirty-five cases of beriberi. It's all too, too terrible. Tired now—more later.

25 April 1942

Very busy since last entry. Stacks of visitors, presents (chocs, tomato juice and cigs—most precious bits there are here—'twas real friendship) and notes. Felt very good—people really are kind. Katherine and Marion outstanding. From hospital can hear your bugle every night. It seems so near. Darling, why can't we get together—but no grumbling. It will not last too long and it could have been much worse. Am sorry for those who ran away. Night not too hot but they gave me a sleeping draught. Luckily Elsie Bullock, a sister I knew before (friend of the Strays), was admitted with the same trouble. They're not sure what it is and are testing everything. Difficult, as body has gone cussed. Today for first time in mature life was given an enema. The tube broke in the middle and splashed everything and I thoroughly enjoyed self. This morning Elsie and I were transferred to upstairs ward (more serious) and we now feel very important. Downstairs more fun in a way—old Mrs Baker crippled with arthritis but her tongue like a speedy safety razor. Daisy (Desirée), and American epileptic of about twenty, hairy body and smells to high heaven—so does her mother who visits her daily—always in the same dress. Mrs X, a Malay who's been constipated for a month, Mrs Wickett a seventy-year-old darling full of rheumatism who picked up Mrs Byrne (Eurasian who looks like Pocohontas) to be her personal maid. Then Mrs Rippon, Chinese-Eurasian wife of a handsome Malacca lawyer, with her six-month-old son who looks whiter than the whitest. On the other side Mrs Bidwell, seventy-two, voice like a man's, mind like a child's, and one passion—cigarettes. Then two I don't know, next a 'lydy' with haemorrhoids and a dreadful

(46)

accent, Elsie and me, then a tearsome wench with sores and Eunice Austen-Hofer (one of the ten from the tool-shed and nice), very good looking, fortyish, stud owner, not the jail-bird type, in with kidneys. That was the lower ward. Upper will follow after forty winks. G'night ... So, nice long sleep, more visitors, food, only very slight temperature and now a cigarette. Good. Oh, knew there was something important— spent long time yesterday sketching your wrinkles into the photo that the efficient Mr Wong had made so pretty, and now you're quite yourself. Am delighted with you and Mother smiles her approval too. Blast it, how in the world would it influence the British or Japanese cause if we were together? I want you so.

27 April 1942

Aches and pains almost all gone but as washed out as soaking cotton wool. However life not too unpleasant at all. The sisters here have all been swell and Elsie and I get great comfort out of swapping symptoms. There are four or five dysentery cases with commodes next to their beds. At lunchtime yesterday the atmosphere was a bit thick so we took our plates and ventured down. Felt like conquerors on our return. Delightful too that the MO has put us on all sorts of odds and ends including Vitamalt which is beautifully sticky. The gang has rallied round and *Pow-Wow* is coming out as usual. (Ethel seems decidedly dangerous.) Hope to get out of here tomorrow or the next day.

28 April 1942

Just another day in hospital but feeling much better, though depressed as hell. A year ago around now you were up Camerons and came back to a go of dengue. This year we seem to be in a slight pickle, yet much prefer it to twelve months ago. Don't you? (Golly, someone in the Men's Camp is playing a saxophone—wonder how he got it in—sounds good.) Oh, choice scandal today. Glover [Edward, editor of the *Malaya Tribune*] and his Julienne were never married. Wife wouldn't divorce him. Wonder what the situation is now?

29 April 1942

Today is the Japanese Emperor's birthday and at ten o'clock everyone had orders to face a certain direction. Two minutes' silence was ended by all the chains being pulled. To celebrate the occasion a box of Rinso was given to every four women and a tin of pineapple to every three. The sentries are in rotten humour (possibly because they must work on their holiday) and bashed Lady Thomas and a couple of others. I lie in bed enjoying life. Have been ordered massage for ye olde backe, and purr like a buffalo in absolute delight. Am a darned fool—worry so much about your reactions to being a POW. Envisage the most horrible developments—well, physically have grounds for worrying, you're being underfed, there's dysentery, malaria and your old lumbago, but otherwise— but if this bunch of women can keep their chins up enough to pull the chains, it surely won't affect you. Must pull myself together or will start underestimating that man Bloom again. My goodness, people are nice. The massage woman brought a violet-ray machine in from Myako and this afternoon surprised me with a ten-minute dose. All the comforts of the General Hospital. Am begining to like this place.

(48)

Just as well had those joyous sentiments last night. Told this morning must stay in a while yet, having various spots of fibrositis (spelling most uncertain) which the masseuse must break down. Have written to Katherine to bring in the yellow bathing suit which still isn't completed. Be dreadful to be released from here with that still undone. Hope you like it. Will probably gain so much weight in hospital that it won't fit. Lie in bed, eat, sleep and write. Disgusting but have no desire to read and a constant urge to write—stories, articles, leaders, even poems and must control self not to fill this notebook to you in one swoop. Will put it away again till later. Now after visiting hours. Seems the atmosphere in the Camp is not so good; reaction to all the grand rumours that floated in last week. Also whole set of new sentries caused by incident in the Men's Camp—guard offered to buy a bottle of whisky for some men. While they were haggling over the price somebody swiped the bottle. Guard very irate and even $45 given by men to placate him didn't succeed and he drew his bayonet and slashed one of them across the face—serious injury—incident reported—guard got two years but no one knows whether for selling whisky or slashing and no one knows who got away with the bottle of whisky. S'funny. Curious to hear from you how the men reacted to the sudden absence of alcohol. My urge is for icecream—have become a sissy—have daydreams of us shopping and exploring through London, stopping every half-hour for mountains of icecream (chocolate). It'll be good fun shopping because there won't be much money and we'll need such a lot. Almost anything will be a necessity because we won't have it. Hope that we are released at the same time to share all the thrills. Alone it wouldn't be any fun.

This is May Day—can think of many I'd like to crown. We had no celebration which was unusual since we almost indiscriminately celebrate anything. Katherine came over in a frenzy this morning—she had broken one of the front (upper) teeth off her plate, looked like a school urchin and would have to continue thus indefinitely since Hanna [the dentist] could not repair it. Her dignity is gone for ever. Heard guns this morning—wonder what they were. Also heard that Keith Simmons [an Army friend] is in one of the warder's houses, solitary, because one of the Tommies beat up a sentry. Doesn't sound plausible. Our sentries socked two more women. Ethel came over, not to see me, and looked most run down, has boils all over her. Doctors have ordered her into hospital but she prefers to break down. Her dislike of me is becoming really pathetic and almost pathological again. Am anxious to get out of hospital but dread returning to her. Am almost thankful to have a rotten back. Darling, will never joke about your lumbago again.

2 May 1942

Two months today since you drove off from Fullerton. It's been pretty bad being separated but otherwise was prepared to face far worse—weren't you—or is yours very, very terrible? However, still don't like it. Don't like any part of the blinking war. Want peace and you and civilisation. Have had one serious new conviction; always felt that moral power decided moral issues and gave moral satisfaction. Material ends were attained by material means. Wars were won partly by the zeal behind them but mostly by cold efficiency and equipment. The land with ten tanks won the battle with the land with only two, but I am now convinced that moral issues enter into the result in no small way. My arguments are not quite straight yet. Someday when they are worked out, will tell them to you and you will smile and say, 'But that's just what I told you over and over again.' You'll be right too. Last night had a long conversation with MacDonald (remember Ward 6 Fullerton, smallish, unhappily married, nice-looking with little affectations). The woman, now thirty-five, is still trying to cope with life using the thoughts that were handed her when she was adolescent. Small wonder she finds it difficult! And gosh, she does fuss as a sister. Have really had enough hospital. Feel no worse than almost anybody else and just being here won't cure my back. Will talk to Dr Worth [Helen, known as Robbie] seriously this morning. 'Twill be funny to leave this ward—along one wall a beautiful Eurasian girl and a nondescript woman with scared eyes, both with breast cysts. Then Miss Dalton, formerly head of Robinson's women's department. Fourteen stone ten of self-possessed woman who now gives the feeblest squeaks: she's down with laryngitis and has turned out to be good fun. Then a nasty bit of chronic invalid, fiftyish, and a moral blackmailer who goes coy and kittenish when she wants something. Next to her an amazing creature, Mrs Walford, looks European but talks incessantly, in the most Eurasian voice ever heard. She tells fortunes and believes herself to be psychic. Remember Mrs Beck, thin, slow-speaking, white-haired, Japanese speaking? She is now recovering from a bad go of dysentery, was not expected to live but is now busy fighting everybody's battles again. She often comes and sits on my bed and we discuss Life with a capital L and she makes rude noises. Opposite are some now empty beds, then an old dear, half paralysed, who caught dysentery. One side of her is completely useless and I wonder whether she has only half the normal diarrhoea. Next me, and then a young, (query) appendix who copies recipes into a notebook all day long. Miss Elsie Bullock who was good fun. My goodness, my gracious, I am excited. Was told this morning out of the blue that they were going to take me to hospital to X-ray my back. Most thrilled. My back will be OK but will have a chance to see all sorts of things and mebbe—oh dear, anything is possible. Can't go today as was thought at first but probably Monday or Tuesday—whoopee!

4 May 1942

Still in hospital and getting fed up with it, though something seems to happen every day. Yesterday there was another funeral, a man, and since his wife had no friends, Ethel as Red Cross went and had a fine time. Bought bread and heard rumours and saw people. Everybody would do almost anything to get out. The death was a pity. Man, forty-five, perforated stomach ulcer, died simply because of lack of nursing. Last night there was a meeting of all the sisters and matrons—would they be willing to go out and nurse? Much discussion, still no decision, my bet is no action will be taken.

9 May 1942

Long time since last entry but—my goodness, don't know where to begin. Spent a couple of days with dengue depression which was topped by Ethel being brought in with a terrific carbuncle. She was very low, is better and we are most friendly. Why not? But—yesterday I was taken to KK [Kadang Karban Hospital] for an X-ray. Darling, we have such good friends and I was so lucky. [I went out padded with letters from all the Army wives to their husbands hoping to meet someone to whom I could pass them. It worked like a dream.] As to Singapore it looked much as before, what I saw of it, scarred but unchanged. Except for a lack of motor traffic the streets had hardly altered. Watching the Chinese, Indians,

Malaya at their simple pastimes one wondered what the excitement had been about and why we were now locked away, parted. There must have been atrocities but I somehow felt that the natives were torn between fear of Japanese beatings and fear of our returning and taking them out of their leading positions. We few (four women and six men) who went in the ambulance were treated absolutely royally. Everybody without exception seemed delighted to see us and could not do enough for us. We had lunch in the nurses' quarters—table set with white cloth, napkins, bread-and-butter plates—it was gloriously civilised. Winchester [Dr] and I wallowed. Sheers [Eurasian doctor, who recently became President of Singapore] could not have been nicer. Spoke to Sai Poh [Goh Sai Poh, very dear Chinese friend, wife of a Chinese doctor], met others and sent you my love. It all made this dengue business so worth while. Almost felt that I should have been sicker to deserve it. Came back so excited couldn't stop talking and slept all today, except when they wounded my dignity by giving me an injection in my bottom (I don't know what). They can do whatever they ruddy well want—yesterday was worth it. Oh, but there are so many things I want to talk to you about—could hear your bugle particularly clearly tonight—prison has given me a new insight into people and situations—how one appreciates those that are sterling—how I appreciate you!

10 May 1942

Darling—spent most of today thinking—really not thinking but feeling—it was good. Six months ago would have hated to die because nothing seemed straight. Today I do not want to die but if I did things would be clear. Because they're clear I know that our lives together will be right. Am glad we went through this war together. Am glad we showed no fear. Am sorry we lost some of our things because they were beautiful but remember your thought that man-made beauty cannot be destroyed—man can make more—and I have seen much beauty since I am here. Am glad of the joy I find in writing—not this letter to you but thoughts that require work and most of all am glad of us. Am surprised at how little Mother worries me. Somehow the knowledge that there is nothing one can do has really sunk in deeply. Was oppressed till now by the awful waste of this imprisonment, but realise that they could hardly let out a few and letting out all would do more harm than good. There is nothing for it but to sit back and wait. It must not be hard. Just now I want to get out of hospital. Good night.

13 May 1942

Am out of hospital and back in the tool-shed. It's good, though the noise resounding on the concrete is amazing. Kate and Katherine are marvellous—get me breakfast in bed and won't let me work. Everybody else is most kind too. On top of that got two shipments of bread and fruit in from outside—an unexpected friend, Mrs Cornelius, whom we knew to be in Changi, is back but had strict orders to tell us nothing. It was most reassuring to see her looking so well. Am no longer so worried. As long as you get enough food and stay well. Got *Pow-Wow* out today—very glad didn't miss a number in spite of being in bed.

19 May 1942

Many days since the last entry. It was hard to find one's way back into Camp life. Then all one's possessions had to be inspected and thought about. The looted frocks fit even better now that I've lost more weight and, oh, the joy of looking at my pictures. Feel brilliant to have salvaged them. Had some very pleasant experiences. In General Hospital there was a refugee patient who seemed most unhappy. Whenever I went to the johnny would pop in and see her. She was still a walking patient when I went to Myako and seemed pleased to see me. Since then she has regularly sent in packages of fruit, bread, chocolates. One loaf was hollowed and contained ten cigarettes. Once she sent some honest-to-goodness meat sandwiches. There was a near riot in the room. Whatever glee one finds in an internment camp is definitely not due to the food. (We have had fresh meat three times since Fullerton Building, about three bites each, no fresh fish and scarcely any vegetables.) You can imagine the excitement then when my illicit parcels arrive per ambulance. And guess what! Saipoh sent me in some homemade biscuits and apricots yesterday, goodness knows how. Ethel had a letter from D [her husband, Denis] but since she does not care for me I was told naught. She's still in hospital. Hope she stays there. This ruddy back keeps me down a good deal and have much time to think (incidentally have a bunged-up tube, get daily douches, a course of contramine—spelling uncertain—injections and may even wangle a regular chair—hope it won't keep me from breeding—anyway you'll fix that). Have thought out that it's time we agitated to get out of this prison to work among the people. Simple things. Teaching them, nursing them, helping them. We must. We told them to put their trust in us. We let them down. Now we must risk whatever they are risking. If it's safe for them it's safe for us. If it's not safe for them we ought to be out to help and share. How can we expect their allegiance later if we don't stick by them now? We can't use this argument with the Japs but there are others and they should be used now.

Ages since last entry—will jot down main developments. We
have had to shift our quarters. There had often been talk of
vacating the tool-shed to make room for the old women (over
sixty-five and pretty helpless). Now it has happened.
Reason—they are bringing in the last of the people who are
out and the men are so overcrowded that they shifted the
women's hospital and by doubling up in the cells transferred
the hospital to what had been a dormitory. The place is much
too small, lacks ventilation and is generally a shambles. God
knows what would happen in case of an epidemic. Feel rather
sorry for Ethel who is still in. Otherwise despise her lying,
sneaking, selfish ways—not because of her but because she has
made such a farce of the Red Cross. She started a Corner at
which women could buy things other women had made or did
not want. That was good, it helped keep them busy and
supplied them with necessities. But all was worked on a cash
basis. Big profits (30%–300%) were collected and also cash
donations. She made speeches in which she ran down Stringer
[Brigadier Charles Stringer, in charge of Army Medical
Services in Malaya] and HE [His Excellency, the Governor]
by name. She literally drooled over every Japanese sentry. She
smeared her personality over everything, pasting it down with
more lies. But she did not do a darn thing to get Red Cross
comforts into the Camp. She did try to organise a shopping
tour to buy embroidery cotton, clothes hangers, etc. with some
of the cash she had collected (about $5000). Steps were taken
to see that cash that may be used for buying food some day be
not frittered away senselessly now. An entertainment was
arranged by Red Cross Corner. It was like the other
entertainments—good considering the material available. By
exerting charms she got permission to give part of the show to
the Men's Camp but she did not manage a single thing about
seeing that five hundred women had a decent room to be used

(56)

as a hospital. I admire her initiative and I know she's bats but can't forgive her for making a joke of the strongest organisation—the only organisation—to help us. Her remark about the stars was typical. Some days ago we were told that Okasaki (the Camp Head) had requested that we embroider four thousand flashes, three stars to each, for his army. Oh, the arguments. Some would not lift a finger for the s. o. b. Others said they saw no harm in it. After much discussion a vote was taken, eighty-nine in favour, a hundred and twenty-seven against. The following day Okasaki sent the flashes in: it was no longer a request, it was an order. So we're all doing flashes. But Ethel told O, for all the world to hear, that she was very sorry about it. He should have given the flashes to her and she and Lady Heath would have seen to it that they were done. Well I felt that the flashes were too petty a point for us to flaunt our principles. Sewing them would not help their army in the slightest. It might make them better disposed to the thousands completely in their hands. The whole thing was too silly to be worth an issue. But one does not let down the decisions or actions of one's own people. She's just a blooming stool pigeon and not worth the two pages wasted on her. Wish she'd get a boil on the end of her tongue.

31 May 1942

Am slipping to write so much yet so little of our new quarters. From the first I yelled, shouted and disclaimed that I'd put up with jail but that nothing would get me into a cell. Well, now we were faced with almost no alternative and I was ready to fight, unreasonably and pigheadedly. There was a small side verandah and I would live there. The Japs had said no one would be allowed to. The Committee had said so too but I damned well was going to—no cell for me. I'd been most co-operative, hardworking, pleasant, etc. but I wasn't going into a cell. Then had a bright thought—would officially share a cell with Katherine (who was thoroughly scared of my unexpected temperament), would leave some bits and pieces there but would really live on the verandah. If anyone said anything would say I live in a cell, am just spending the day down. Diplomacy, dissembling at its best. Very satisfied. So together we heaved our boxes and cases up to cell 30AIV on the second floor. Horrible place. Seven foot by ten and a three foot by six slab of concrete, eighteen inches high, down the centre. On one side an Asiatic squatter. A tiny window, one foot by four foot ten, up in the ceiling. Really awful. To hide the slab (most mortuary like) decided to build some shelves and K and I went about swiping every plank we could see. The shelves were quite successful. Then we thought we could use the two end walls as dressing table space. We stole, sawed and hammered more wood. Covered same with coloured towels, your picture, Mother's, bottles and mirror, comb and brush. Not bad. Oh—when we left the tool-shed our bedding, mattress and beds were debugged. Don't know how they did it but they now smell awful and I have grave suspicions. They must have taken my bed apart, for it came back about two feet wide but four feet high. The mattress won't balance on it. So wrapped the prison-made bedspread round the mattress and arranged it on the suitcases to make a divan; quite comfortable. The bed I left on the verandah. And then looked so determined that so far they've been afraid to say a word. Also installed *Pow-Wow* office and a dining table on the verandah and we really are well organised. The joke of it all is that I now love our cell because it is private (honest) and not too ugly—but cannot admit that to anyone but Katherine. We don't spend very much time up there but the hours we have we thoroughly enjoy. Kate has moved in with Marion. They make a most extraordinary but successful combination. Katherine and I are really very busy now. She does the housework while I do *Pow-Wow* and we both do four hours a day as VADs, not in the regular hospital but taking care of the old ladies. It's most amusing and we like it. It's good to be healthy again. Still get injections but have put on weight and am a hundred and twenty pounds again. Look awful when less than that. Within a day or so am starting collecting Camp statistics and this week we began meetings to discuss reconstruction of all and any social problems. Am disappointed because all the other Army wives have had direct messages but consider it a small price for marrying a man who's brilliant but impractical. Came in full of feelings about you that still come over me in waves, but thought that feelings alone were not enough to last a long internment. Have now mentally found you completely. Your faults have become as familiar as my own, until now I not only condone them but admire them. And as to your virtues—well, darling, am trying hard to develop into something deep and fine enough to be worthy of you.

8 June 1942

Have stage-fright. Am due to give a lecture on 'Reformation Work' to the Camp at 8.45 and have already started to stutter and stammer. There used to be entertainments every Friday evening but since they have started 8.30 blackouts (which means no lights) again, we have three a week. Either lectures or music. Tonight it's my turn and hate the idea. Wish you were here to tell me not to be an ass. Our social problems supper last night was a success, though women seem incapable of sticking to a topic or remaining impersonal. One cannot tell what the outcome of this war will be but reconstruction must crop up in the brains of all who think. Sometimes feel that if England regains Malaya it might be fun for us to stay on—or rather to return. There are so many worse countries and having stuck it out so far one does feel slightly possessive.

We'll see. Rather amusing Cicely Williams (a sincere woman doctor and charming woman) and I planned these Sunday suppers. Our first idea was to get the whole Camp in on discussions of coming problems but the reactions were not very encouraging. So we decided to use only twelve of the brightest females—invitation only—very snob. This morning the entire Camp was in a furore. Why wasn't so and so asked and why not she? Every ten minutes some woman would stroll up and start some blinking conversation, apropos of nothing, to convince me of her intellectual prowess. Rival groups are being started—all to the good. Our object was to make people think and they are thinking with a vengeance. Goodness knows how long it will last. Today even our old ladies got on to it. Must now go wash for lecture. Goodbye and wish me luck.

9 June 1942

Well, the lecture was neither a howling success nor a dismal failure. In the middle of it I got terribly fed up with the sound of my own voice and stopped but everyone asked intelligent questions so I continued and finished it. People applauded, said it was most interesting and thank you so much and then we all went to bed. I much relieved that it was over.

Today I am thrilled to the core. Remember we went to Mrs Bateman's [Angela Bateman, well-known local artist] exhibition at Raffles and I didn't like it much (she was off on her colour)? Well Mrs B was very ill shortly after internment and spent months at Myako returning here about a week ago. She has agreed to my studying and working with her and will even lend me some of her brushes and paints. She can teach me so much—it's very good indeed. Have done a few things but unsatisfying—had only charcoal that I burnt myself. But now—!

What a day! What a wonderful, fine day. Victor H sent over
some super pastels and a thermos—ours was broken and, now
that we do the old ladies, Katherine and I eat an hour after
everyone else so a thermos is just what's needed.

19 June 1942

Many days have passed with no urge to write but today—oh,
darling Philip, darling—want to write reams, volumes, tomes
but can't sit still long enough to write a word—you're well,
you're miserable, you're mine—if you knew what it meant to
read those precious, precious lines both so entirely and
completely you [a letter from Philip had been smuggled into
the Camp]. Not a practical, material point in them—just a cry
from you to me—and that's all I wanted. Do you know,
sweet, until today I had often felt that I was yours and I rolled
in the warmth of the feeling but today I know, know, *know*
that you're mine. How that makes one grow. Oh, my darling,
at first was just a little bit sorry that your life and interests
remained pretty much the same. Thought it would have been
better if you had no batman and if my spoiled Philip would
have to chop wood, clean, sew and queue for his food.
Thought that mingling with as motley a crowd as we have
here would give you something that would lead to greater
happiness for you eventually. Now am glad—am too jealous of
every trait, virtue and fault, that make up you. Just stay
healthy, husband mine, and continue hating it. I'll try to make
up for every miserable moment you have now.

Katherine too had a message—full of minute detail. And
Marion a long screed. How our humours have changed. Two
days ago K had a birthday and we really got off a fine
celebration with masses of 'unusual' presents. That day we
were allowed to send official messages to you. A good day too.

Today, for all things come at once, they told us to prepare

(61)

for postcards to our families. Rumour persists that we will be
moved from here. Please no! Have even finished the yellow
bathing suit.

20 June 1942

Have had a lovely time today thinking of all the various ways
our lives might go when we get together again. What a variety.
First of all it may be a very, very long time till you are
demobilised and we might develop into an Army couple; that
is we might lead Armyish lives. Perhaps in some occupied
territory, who knows? We might go home and you work on a
special degree; we'd live in two rooms and be very poor but
we'd enjoy life. You might try your old practice again and it
would be tough going for a few years. You might go into
partnership with another doctor—either London or near some
other big city. Perhaps we'll decide to stay on in Malaya—
there are worse places. South Africa might call, though I
cannot see you yet completely returning to the fold, though
the warmth of a large family might be grand. And we might
even throw over the traces and try America. So many
alternatives yet each one fun in spite of its own drawbacks.

Oh, Philip, it is good to know that no matter what the world
situation may be we'll get the most out of life because we're
together. Nothing else matters. That's why I don't mind this
internment at all. Individuals have always had to pay the price
of international wars. Too bad but a fact. If our price is a year
or two of separation it's not too much, for this war also gave
me you. And nothing else matters—so to bed.

The last ten days have had an unbelievable spurt of efficiency probably due to complete peace of mind where there had been so many worries. Anyway have been writing (*Pow-Wow* and endless chits that were cast upon the waters), doing statistics (average age of the women is forty-two years, eight months, there are three hundred and seventy-seven in all, of which eighty-eight are Eurasian and about a dozen pure Asiatics) and sewing like mad. Feel that it is most urgent that all my things are in order in case of (a) a sudden move and (b) a very long stay here. Near the Old Hospital (think I mentioned that it was moved to make room for the men) there was a room with a busted lock marked 'STRICKLY NO AD-MISSION'. Inside were the prisoners' private clothes and there I 'found' some fine Chinese coolie jackets and pants and also some trousers. The jackets are really rather smart and I have set a new fashion, the pants could be altered into shirts, shorts and even a skirt. Not all are a success but it's fun. During the mornings usually wear khaki shirts and shorts (the latter a gift from the Men's Camp). Change into a frock in the afternoons or evenings (darned lucky to have looted that stuff in Fullerton). One looks so pasty-faced here that one must spend as much thought as possible on one's appearance. Everybody, incidentally, envies me my two pairs of gum-soled shoes—they stand up so well to the concrete. Often wonder what you are doing about footwear. Amusing the things that become problems or rarities in internment. Elizabeth Ennis and her cellmate got a chair the other day—a real honest-to-goodness one, with a back and arms and everything. Visit them now just to sit. Only the crippled and the pregnant have chairs here and you cannot imagine how one's back aches for support sometimes. One never gets used to either sitting up or lying down. Also I would like to eat something with a fork—this constant rice with soup of some description makes me spoon conscious. Furthermore I want to see a tree and I want to sit in a bathtub and just now I would like you to kiss me — not too lightly.

Camp news — ardent elections, with Ethel making a darned fool of herself. Unfortunately there have been signs of her old trouble and I can no longer dislike her but again feel worried. Why, goodness only knows, she's not my responsibility but there it is. Rather enjoy my position here; have steadfastly refused to join any committees or stand in any elections but being intimate with those in power I exert considerable influence — (*Pow-Wow* is a camp institution of no little importance). The role of power behind the throne tickles my vanity no end and also has some very practical advantages. The doctors are undoubtedly the leaders here. One or two are fools but Eleanor Hopkins is very good value. Cicely Williams has a great deal to her and 'Robbie' Worth and Margaret Smallwood are good fun. The sisters almost without exception are very anti-doctor and some of the criticism is really extraordinary. In much the same way the teachers are most critical of the other teachers and the mems of the other mems. I really think this place is fun.

10 July 1942

And today am just fed up with it. Have had quite enough and want out. Didn't want to be separated on the 7th. [My birthday is 6 February, Philip's is 7 November. To give us a celebration between the two, we chose 7 July as 'our day'.] Wanted to give you things and make things for you and see you looking pleased. Balls to it all. Have been down ever since. Oh, and fun — today a woman came in with a message from you. I am to go straight to my folks here — she thought she had it slightly mixed up. Slightly? On the 4th of July the Americans celebrated Independence Day which thoroughly

(64)

amused me. Eight of us had a picnic supper on the lawn—hot
dogs, vegetable salad, fruit and pink lemonade. All watching
faces drooled and dribbled. One passer-by asked, 'Who does
what and with which and to whom?' Another suggested
Interdependence Day. You should have seen the eight—two
Methodist missionaries, one spoiled Methodist missionary
(now living with another woman's husband—that is BC
[Before Changi]), one mixture who claims her father's
nationality (and who's to say her nay?), one Spanish girl born
in NY while her parents were travelling and two 'just wives'
who were caught here. There's another, wife of Bailey of
Cowan and Bailey, but she doesn't like us. Rumours recently
have been too good. Just when Libya was almost lost again,
the tide turned. The Americans are practically in Singapore
and the Russians are holding out. The women expect to be let
out by the middle of August but since we're here they expect
to be let out the middle of next month. It keeps them going.
This week our captors have been bad-tempered, or as they
term it, restless. All communication with the Men's Camp has
been stopped and the ambulance may no longer bring in extra
food, etc. A Captain James, liaison officer, is said to be
responsible. 'Tis a sad but true fact that most of our greatest
discomforts are caused not by the enemy but by our own folk.
Witness Charlie [Charles Stringer]. Do so want to know how
he got his soul besmirched. Time for lights out—see you
later.

15 July 1942

Last night we were permitted to listen to a concert given by
the men. Most unexpected for there had been hell to pay for
two days. The women, though warned repeatedly that they
were not allowed to speak, signal or otherwise contact the
males, found it too much for them and some insisted upon

clinging to the bars most zoologically and giving vent to their
repressed appetites. In a fury Tokuda [one of the two
Japanese officers in charge of the Camp] had some of the
grilles boarded up and with much shouting closed all points of
contact. The women said it was another example of Oriental
mental cruelty. Having heard tales of Chinese atrocities and of
the seven Malay heads staked at various points of town, I
thank our fates for such cruelty as we had been forced to
endure. The women remain a constant source of wonder to
me. I hope I never become entirely British, for then I could
not appreciate them. The concert was most entertaining —
many of the turns we had seen together at Victoria Theatre
and I could easily feel that you were still sitting next to me. It
suddenly struck me how dreadful it must be for Kate, most of
the nursing sisters and others who have no one to whom they
can look forward. To think of getting out to nothing is just
too ghastly. All day long I have been filled with pity — feeling
mighty, mighty rich. Incidentally, just recently sex is
beginning to make itself felt, nothing visibly lesbian but a
number of hysterical outbursts. Am told that the rice diet has
damped the men's spirits no end. Re sex, feel exceedingly
sorry for one nursing sister who in the heat of war became
careless and is now in her sixth month. Tough. Wish I could
change places with her. Forgot to tell you last Saturday's
amusing incident with a sentry. He was ordered to take ten
Free French with their seven days' rations to the pier to catch
a boat to Saigon. That evening he returned. Yes, he had
obeyed orders and delivered them. The boat unfortunately
had left before their arrival so he just left them on the pier and
there, for all we know, the ten Free French and their seven
days' rations still are. Darling, do you look at the sky much
where you are? It's become such an important part of my
life — it's so very beautiful. Am glad you haven't got walls.
Hate them very much. People say that this has taught them
how simply one can live. I don't agree. Every day feel anew

how much beauty, comfort, being civilised means. Don't like this. Am quite willing to work, work hard but I don't like this. We both don't like this and we're never going to have anything like it again. Goodnight, Philip, I love you.

10 August 1942

Long time since the last entry—will have a hard time catching up. Just three weeks ago rushed upstairs to the cell to dress for breakfast. And there promptly fainted. Must have knocked head on concrete for landed in hospital with concussion. Further examination revealed reflexes that wouldn't reflect, haemoglobin under sixty and blood pressure under a hundred. The inelegant quality of the food had got me down. Slept straight through the first fortnight, then was transferred to what is called the Hospital Annexe—some beds on a breezy verandah—where I am beginning to enjoy life again. Was annoyed at letting so silly a thing knock me down when others far less sturdy continued but there 'tis. And once again am staggered at how extraordinarily kind people are. Katherine I will not describe now for you'll hear lots about her when we meet—you cannot imagine her untiring thoughtfulness. Get something to eat every two hours and she breaks her head trying to think of nice things. Wasn't allowed to read or write so she played endless silly card games with me. She is a very good guy. The doctors too (Robbie Worth and Eleanor H) have been swell. Cooley, the funny little man from upstairs, sent me milk out of the blue. Bob (Jean's) sent cod liver oil. Hock (the policeman) sent coconuts. Men and women—all have been just elegant. Bob even built me a most civilised bed. You need never worry about me—people always are just too good. If only I could be assured that you are among as good a crowd. Tomorrow must tell you about how the police came to see me. Big stuff! Goodnight, darling.

11 August 1942

Day before yesterday was in most inelegant position filing
toenails when lo and behold the Garrison Commandant and
two who had obviously taken honours degrees from the
Gestapo, Ogpu and Scotland Yard stood at my bed. Where
were *Pow-Wow* files, papers, etc. and how about searching my
cell? Told them where *Pow-Wow* hung out and that there was
naught in my cell and that I had a headache. Then off to the
office, guided by Katherine, where they took away all our bits
and pieces including my typewriter and a box of scrap paper
we used as bumpf. They must 'investigate' same. Whole
schlemozzle because some misguided woman, while a patient
at Myako, sent her friend (Eurasian) a letter including *Pow-
Wow* and both fell into Japanese hands. Since our paper is
absolutely and utterly above board and has from the word go
refused to discuss politics in any shape, all is well. But want
my typewriter back; the two intelligence men should be
reminded that under the present regime people can be
decapitated for looting and surely they would not want that.
The woman has been removed to CID headquarters and we
are all most worried about her welfare. The camp wants *Pow-
Wow* and I continue happily lying in bed drinking gallons of
milk (we got a big Klim). In the meantime much talk about
repatriation. Mebbe so, mebbe not. What's the good of
worrying? Have enough wondering about your welfare.

12 August 1942

Last night was most terribly blue; know now that it was just
p.m. depression and it's all over—just one bit remains and
that is the recognised knowledge that should anything happen
to me (stupid phrase—should I die) before we get together, it
doesn't really matter. It would be a pity, for the story should

have its 'and they lived happily ever after' ending, but having had you, and the rest of my life such as it was, there was a completeness, a Platonic beginning, middle and end that can leave no regrets. However do not intend to die, not without having had many years with you—p.m. depressions and all. Reading a good book *Quest for Corvo* by Symons. And from tomorrow on will have a private secretary to take down and type stories, etc. What a life of ease—luverly. Darling, bound up with my love for you is an urge to write well. It's so strong the whole lot of it.

14 August 1942

Up and about yesterday and feeling like a human being again. Beriberi knocked for six and all else improving. Much talk of repatriation. Still hate the idea but am becoming slightly reconciled. Am not much good to you wrecked. Can do nothing in here and many other sensible arguments but, oh heck, didn't stay behind to be repatriated. One will see—incidentally they say that Singapore was bombed yesterday. Am very much against that. 'They say' that Nimura was one of a party that came round two days ago (parties are always strolling through gazing at us à la Whipsnade) and was horrified at our conditions (especially the men who are horribly overcrowded—a hundred in a room the size of a tennis court). He asked for a sample tiffin which that day was particularly foul and was more horrified. Don't know whether all this is true but yesterday there were terrific rations of meat (perhaps it was horse—anyway, it was a lot) and the same are due today. You must, must, must take care of yourself.

22 August 1942

Darling, this diary is a wash-out. It does not give a picture of this Camp but more of a hospital bulletin. Will try jotting down memorable occasions or happenings and explain them to you when we are together. Am still in hospital but all better (wish there was a table to write on).

A week ago Sir Shenton [the Governor] and his party left. There were military on board too but, I am told, no majors. Thank goodness. Repatriation is still in the air. They have replaced the Jap sentries with Sikh policemen. Another sop and a slap. More talk about a second front being opened. Tut, tut! Nuts to world news. Changi life is amusing. Our little *kongsi* [group] (Marion, Kate, Katherine and I) still gets along well. For talks and fun there's Katherine plus Eleanor and Robbie and often Cicely. Much laughter at silly situations. Remind me to tell you of the night K cleaned somebody else's teeth, about Helen Dives's appetite and the swiped cake, also about the third helping, passionate Iris and the coconut, sick husband and fatherless children, the Methodist missionary (Miss Rank) enquiring whether Mrs Dickie's show was 'shady'. The awful situation with Miss Rank while Marion delivered a lecture on how she developed her bust.

23 August 1942

Three years ago today landed in Malaya. Another girl who came out on the same boat and I are celebrating tonight. 'Scrazy but I am happier today (this in spite of hearing motor horns outside all afternoon—they do make me feel so hemmed in). Gosh, darling, how I want you. Don't think this desire could ever go stale even if they keep us here for years and years. I do hope they don't; we'd be so unattractive at the end of that time. My illness depressed me terribly a month ago—

looked so awful. Now with all the sunshine of the annexe, plus Vit. B injections, plus weight, am full of beans and an urge to get together. My hunch is that we will not be together till autumn next year—can't see it any sooner, can you? But who knows. Anyway, everybody has a hunch! Want one too. A ship from SA [South Africa] brought soup, maize and nasty sweets. Do hope you got lots. The men are playing cricket— one can hear the noise over the walls. Am doing an illustrated series on Changi birds—fun.

25 August 1942

The anniversary celebration was quite good. Anna Robertson (who came out on the *Ranchi* with me), Robbie Worth (her sister, my MO and pal), Eleanor Hopkins and of course Katherine. Toby Williams and Kate came uninvited. Anna had made a cake of rice, coconut, *gula malacca* [a sweet, fudge-like substance much like brown sugar]. It was very delicious. Kath made coffee and swiped some cubes from the hospital refrigerator so we had it iced. I had some biscuits and we discussed the double standard in Malaya and generally. Personally don't mind it—think it's the thing that makes being a woman worthwhile, but the doctors and nurses are rabid on the subject. Party broke up around 11 to the shushing of many women who thought us too hilarious. Terrific thunderstorm in the middle of the night. The hospital annexe being a verandah got it full in the face. I had just had a pleasant dream (yes, sir, about you), pulled my green bedspread-cum-macintosh-sheet-cum-bedding-roll over me and wallowed in sleepy, warm, dry comfort when the trickle of rain reminded me of all the iced coffee. It was bad, for the rain was coming down in torrents. There was nothing to be done. If I had been a man might have been ingenious. Wondered whether that was the basis of the double standard and luckily

(71)

fell asleep. Though the woman who sneaked out *Pow-Wow* is back and the paper is coming out as usual the Japanese still have my typewriter — war atrocity. Most annoying.

28 August 1942

Look, darling, new fountain pen. Good, isn't it? Busted the other. Camp still full of repatriation talk. Today a new rumour (renewal of an old) that we are only being moved to St John's Island. Don't believe it. By now want very badly to be repatriated. The old optimistic days (together in six months) have died of undernourishment. If we cannot get together want to be out building at least the foundations of a home for you when you are released. I am of far more use to you out than in and the chances of getting Singapore back shortly seem very slim. Should I tell you of my one big day-dream? That they will repatriate some of the too badly wounded accompanied by a few doctors. That's where you come in. It's far fetched but an awful help. I lie here discussing it with you day in and day out. By the way, did I ever tell you that you're the only person I ever met who uses the word 'thus' as if it were part of modern usage? That methinks is part of the secret of your success. You take whatever you like out of the past and treat it as if it were part of the present. Logical and queer.

1 September 1942

Life is full of surprises. Today I was presented with a douche can. This is really the most illogical jail. Incidentally rumour has killed repatriation. We are now being sent into town somewhere. OK by me. To return to the douche can — am going to start a new business and give enemas or such at two bits a time. We are all running short of cash. Thank goodness we had as much as we did. It's been a godsend. We hear that the officers are not being paid their just (International Law) deserts. The other night had a long talk with Bess Rogers. Funny how people turn out in jail. Everybody was scared to death of her at first, as she was known as 'Spore's prize bitch. Here she has become meek and mild and, surprisingly, a bore of bores. She has become maid-of-all-work to Lady T with whom she and three others spend all their time. They have no interests nor wit and pass the days in shocking banality. Lady T is sweet and charming and completely negative. This internment must be very tough on them. Remember you used to chide me for thinking it important that I was intelligent? Always thought you spoke through your hat. Now wonder whether you weren't referring to something different. Eleanor H is clever; it gives her pleasure which is good but her pleasure seems to be derived more from the evidence of her cleverness than from its existence pure and simple—the things she said—the things she did and the things she is capable of doing. If the intelligence is there its evidence should just be taken for granted. Mebbe 'twas that which annoyed you. Digging for the silver lining—am glad to have this time to work out the things you used to say, still don't agree with all but at least understand 'em. There is, for instance, your argument that we need utter and complete harmony and agreement. Harmony? Yes! No discords? Definitely! Agreement? Not always! Am getting a heck of a lot of enjoyment out of our tiffs in retrospect. Must be a streak of masochism!

4 September 1942

Great excitement last two days. Okasaki and Tokuda left. Asahi came (speaking very good English, former attaché, we are told, of Jap Embassy in London) very polite and determined to stamp out dysentery. We have had none for about two months and agreed heartily. He does not live in but has two resident pipsqueaks. The day before yesterday near riot when a man refused to obey Sikh's orders to count off in threes (said he was civil internee and what the ——). Sikh slapped him. Johns (Men's Commandant) went to lodge complaint to Asahi and pipsqueaks locked him in lavatory (honestly) for four hours. More fun and games when we were suddenly presented with a Siamese Eurasian 'wardress'. We refused to accept her as such, call her 'liaison officer' (she speaks no Japanese) and so far are not too aware of her presence. Rumours last two days very heartening. Yesterday celebrated third anniversary of the war. Please no more! I'm depressed: am not getting full value out of food (all sorts of extras) and still suffering from various deficiencies. Have been in hospital six and a half weeks now which is quite enough. (Oh, remind me to tell you the story of Eunice and the bottle of beer.) Katherine, Cicely and Marg Smallwood are coming round to play bridge—see you later.

5 September 1942

Awfully pleased with life. The other day offered editorship of *Pow-Wow* to Taps [Mrs Taplin]. She said she thought she'd love it but would think it over and let me know in a day. Yesterday (me still blue) she came and hemming and hawing apologising that she didn't feel up to it. I suddenly felt so good. Didn't know I was so fond of the rag but what made it best was the expression on the faces of the women who work with me (Toby Williams, Constance Sleep, Mary Thomas) when they heard we were carrying on as was. We do get along awfully well. Our rows are clear-cut, straight from the heart affairs. 'Sfunny, never expected to like so many women and to enjoy their company so much. Always had one or two good women friends but en masse was scared stiff of them. Still prefer men but respect women much more. Neither really matter very much—but am most glad to be a woman because you're a man and it makes things so much easier.

6 September 1942

Must tell you about the dustbin parade: every day about ten wives carry the Women's Camp dustbins up to the main square where their ten husbands empty them, swill them and return them. Sometimes if the sentries aren't watching they can sneak a hello or even touch hands. There are about one hundred wives with husbands across the way. They all await their dustbin turn eagerly and wear their best frocks and pearls for the event. Today there was pandemonium, for the big Sikh on duty found the responsibility too much and fainted dead away. Delightful scene as twenty happy men and women swarmed around him with helpful advice, quickly exchanging their long stored up news and messages. Repatriation is very high again. By the way can't remember whether I ever mentioned how glad I am that you are not across the way. The overcrowding is ghastly and I would hate to see you surreptitiously over dustbins. The food may not be better in the Military Camp (food now vastly improved) but accommodation for officers is undoubtedly more civilised. God, how I long to see you—but not cooped up here. Katherine got a chart of the skies and we are getting quite good at identifying the various constellations. It's fun.

8 September 1942

Oh boy, darling, you cannot imagine what happened! My goodness am I thrilled. They had an Arts and Crafts celebration. The women's stuff was sent over to the Men's Camp and all judged together. I had only one pastel (night scene) that I had kept. Haven't done anything while in hospital. Sent in the night scene and got—second prize. Am shattered with surprise—there were so many entries—especially from the men. Isn't it fun, Philip? Do wish you were here.

Some hours later—what a good day this has been—before breakfast a drainsweeper looked aghast at something in the flow of the drain. I got out of bed to see and found a sparrow caught in the muck and almost drowned. Got it out, dried it as well as I could, made a bed for it in a towel and let it rest. Managed to feed it a bit from my mouth and this evening it flew away, all better. Did not expect it to live. This is about the sixth bird I (or one of the gang) have rescued but only about the second to recover completely. Good.

11 September 1942

Darling, am depressed today—have spent a lot of time recently figuring out possible peace terms for an early (1943) peace, terms that will satisfy communistic Russia, democratic (?) England and USA, recently socialistic France and non-Fascist Germany and Italy. It's got to be a peace that offers something better than we had and, Philip, the more I think of it the more I realise that we are not ready for it yet. The world cannot stand very much more war, yet we are not qualified for peace—what a mess. What more depresses me is that though all the women (and men) here howl for early deliverance not one is taking the time to sit down and figure things out. Oh, yes—they talk about the reconstruction of Malaya (based mostly on self-righteously kicking out those who left) (I still think that many are here now because they were suckers or scared—but no one will agree—they are a bunch of blooming heroes—they insist) after (naturally) a British victory. And if one asks, 'But what are we going to do about the Germans this time?' they say, 'Castrate them' and laugh delightedly because they've used a dirty word. Ugh, Philip, I'm fed up—will go and eat some of the bramble jelly I won for my picture.

22 September 1942

Great developments—Katherine is out on a job helping Cicely Williams collate our diet charts. It all came quite suddenly and I am delighted that she had the chance to get out. She spends all her time doing things for others—(mostly me) and then gets fits of depression because she has 'accomplished nothing'. This will buck her up no end. Of course I miss her terribly and so does Judy but we manage to console each other. I am out of hospital since last week and darned glad to be back in the swim again. Don't do much and everyone is extremely nice. Incidentally my four men (Duncan Wallace, Hockenhull, Cooley and Hitch) [friends from pre-Changi days now in the Civilian Men's Camp] have turned up trumps and do and send all sorts of cheering bits. Very worried. A few nights ago woke up in a cold sweat of anxiety about you. Do hope it was just rice. Oh, Philip, Philip, please stay well. Another bit of news is that an old dream of mine is finally going to be realised—am producing a circus for the children to be given end of next month. Have two ferocious lions, horses, elephants, trained seal, etc. Toby and I are going to be the clowns. Much Camp scandal—five men bribed a Sikh sentry to be allowed to stay out after fatigues. They returned via a rope at three that night. Unfortunately one was very fat, the rope broke and the Japs caught him. They had been visiting a local kampong. Result: Sikh and men flogged and, I imagine, price of the lady in question went up. And all this on a rice diet.

27 September 1942

We're going, we're not, we are, we're not—each day flutters away like petals off a daisy as repatriation seems either a certainty or an impossibility. This constant fluctuation is very wearing and irritating. I do not much like these days, though each when it has been analysed is full of interest. With Katherine away I mix more with other, new women and it's quite good fun. Mother's birthday was terrific—celebrated with three different parties—I entertained with coffee and dry soda biscuits at elevenses. Toby had a supper party—scrambled eggs and a tin of beetroot. Someone got hold of some shallots and someone else produced a tin of mushrooms—what a meal. And at 9.30 (lights out at 10—and we sat in the moonshine) we had coffee and cake (made from cornflakes, coconut and dates) and an alcoholic drink—honest—we brewed it ourselves from fermented *gula malacca* and raisins. It was very sweet and not very strong but that was because it had not stood long enough. We made a new brew for Christmas which should be excellent. If only we could get together. Will not, must not, think of it.

Camp politics cropped up this week—censorship of my *Pow-Wow*—I most delighted because the Camp became so agitated at the Committee's suggestion that it had to be dropped. I just sat back delighted to see how my battles were being fought for me. Katherine seems to be enjoying herself and Sai Poh (bless her) has sent in her love again.

Main thing is that on the 29th we all went on a bathing party to Tanah Mira (fifteen minutes' walk away). This was the third Camp outing but I had been in hospital for the other two. It was glorious, though we left at 2 and had to be back at 5 (that is 12.30 to 3.30 our time and mighty hot). [When the Japanese took over they had set all clocks to Tokyo time.] Swimming was just as good as it always had been and my yellow bathing suit was a big success. Lying in the sun quite forgot the past seven months and when I saw how little effect it all had had I did not mind going back again. It just seemed a funny joke of a home. Repatriation stock has fallen completely and now there is talk of being allowed out on parole. No details given yet. Would be tempted. Hate the idea of being a Jap prisoner for a year or two without any personal contact with them. Would rather risk the odd unpleasantness and see for myself than play bridge in here. Also if we were allowed to live with friends (Asiatic) without jeopardising their safety, it would be a great improvement, as well as, possibly, an encouragement and help to them. Promise you won't let old independent curiosity lead me into any silliness—will wait and see. The last General Meeting most amusing. Remember skinny Mrs Beck who rowed with the orderlies at Fullerton— she has constant grievances and campaigns here and makes a confounded nuisance of herself. It was decided that as long as I remain Editor of the Camp newspaper there would be no official censorship. Our little white-haired girl. (The perm has grown out of my hair and it's a great nuisance.)

7 October 1942

A Red Cross ship arrived with stores. Marvellous food and cigarettes but now all the women are fighting about them. Wonder whether it's the same in the Military Camp? Katherine seems to be doing well—

8 October 1942

Interrupted—she has sent in one or two things—am most curious to hear what she has to say. The women are now allowed to write to their husbands across the way and we are moving heaven and earth to get the same privilege. Very funny—have your old passport photo and have looked at it and the recent snap so much sometimes get mixed up and imagine you now as you were then. Won second prize in a bridge tournament. Hope I don't develop into the type of woman who always gets second prize. Plans for the circus are going well. For a change both repatriation and parole are down—we just plan to stay here till the end. Incidentally, poor Ethel was allowed no say in the Red Cross stores and is most offended. Tsk, tsk. Bess Rogers has opened a Camp barber shop. Elizabeth Ennis [nursing sister married to a doctor in the Indian Medical Service] does little (they were beastly about the Military sisters) and keeps much to herself. Marion has learned bridge. I am trying to knit and Kate is studying Buddhism.

14 October 1942

Big schlemozzle! There are about four nasty, bitter, frustrated, inhibited bitches here who are always starting trouble and now they're up in arms about the dogs again. We have five dogs on the strength. Well cared-for, well-behaved animals adored by all—except for the few horse-faced faggots who want to kill them. Well, tomorrow we're having a paper vote. Keep or destroy. I know the dogs will win but want it to be an overwhelming majority. You should see Judy—she knows something is up—small wonder! Wherever we go tear-eyed women bend and pat her and say 'Poor Judy, we won't let them hurt you.' The Old Ladies' Annexe said they would barricade themselves in with her if the vote went wrong. Even the doctors are on our side. I know there is no sense in getting sloppy about animals but there is darned little to love in an internment camp and dogs are—dogs.

We got a lot of fruit into the Camp yesterday. Ate enough to get a tummy-ache and thoroughly enjoyed it. The circus is getting on very well.

22 October 1942

Such fun about the dogs. We voted but weren't checked off (because the cards were being used for the oaths). Result three hundred for dogs, thirty against. Complaint from the anti-doggers: some women were seen voting twice. Righto, we vote again, this time an anti-dogger changes the issue into Keep or Send Out to Homes. This is not the real issue so the pro-doggers say vote is null and void. Righto! On Saturday we vote some more. Wotta Camp! In the meantime we all sign papers we won't run away and will obey rules of the Camp. The Japs consider this very important. We look at the height of the walls and the wording of the oath and grin. Also I hear that my friend Duncan Wallace has collected some TB which upsets me greatly. Am trying to feed him up. Thank goodness Helen [his wife who was in America] does not know. Am learning how to knit like fury but it doesn't help much. Am very fed up with this situation, Major Bloom. There is only one thing I want in this world and that's you. Bother the circumstances. It's eight months now—will another eight see us through?

26 October 1942

The dogs won, two hundred and forty to twenty-seven. Good! Just found out that my prison number is 2669. Much movement along the road yesterday. Talk of a Red Cross ship taking away the wounded. Wonder where you are? Circus getting bigger and better every day. There's a real circus family called Palomar in here (mother, father, two daughters, son and son-in-law). At first they scorned our show but now they are the backbone of it. Enjoy them very much. Katherine and Cicely have rowed with their male superintendent. Story sounds most complicated and queer. We are having many air raid practices. Big party last night. Passionate Iris Bolton, very dark wife of one of the warders, was thirty-four. Lady Thomas made a speech. Jill Dawson, Bess Rogers, all the doctors, many black-and-tans were there, forty-two in all, all mixed up and having a wonderful time. Socially, I am a confirmed democrat—politically, no! [What did I mean?] See you later.

29 October 1942

Few days ago Red Cross parcels and letters arrived from SA. The parcels were rifled. Letters told of many who had left. Glover is in India. Changi military seems to be on the move. There are many mosquitoes in Bangkok. Talk that now that Katherine is staying out I should share the cell with someone else. I don't give a damn about anything. The squabbles in this Camp are as expected. All I want is you or out. Out so I can get things ready for you. Never thought it possible to

worry so much about anyone. Can't get you out of my mind —
not for ten minutes. Darling, take care of yourself.

7 November 1942

Your birthday, my darling, if only we were together. Am
looking very terrific in high heels, perfume and finery.
Celebrating like anything. Last night we had the circus and it
was a most terrific success. Everybody's still got a smile. We
might give it to the men. Remind me to tell you about the
Palomars. On the 3rd we sent home postcards and went for a
walk—all in honour of an Emperor's birthday—the greatest
we were told that ever lived. Must be, no other has let me
write a postcard or go for a walk. Since the first we must boil
all our drinking water. Very tiresome. Katherine's coming
back in a week or ten days. Must go celebrate your birthday
some more.

13 November 1942

One day passes after the other. On the whole they pass
quickly. Only sometimes one is overwhelmed with the utter
futility and vacuity of all one's actions. I hate to watch myself
bluffing myself into thinking I'm very busy and not really
minding this separation so terribly. All the Military with few
exceptions are said to have gone to Siam, land of the free and
smells. Perhaps you have gone? If so, by now I am worried
out. There is no more worry left. Darling, take care of
yourself—at least it's not Formosa. One of the men was
caught trying to pass something to the Military. He has been
beaten and is in solitary. The temper of the Japs has been
pretty bad recently. The temper of the internees is not so good
either. There have been incidents. There will probably be

(83)

more. Oh, sweetheart, how one longs for a spot of normality. This is so Alice Through the Looking Glass.

18 November 1942

Haven't thought much of the past week. In spite of the Algerian news and the recapture of Tobruk (*Syonan Times*) the temper of all about is mouldy. I have been kicked in the face by an unexpected source and was slightly boiling for a day or so. All about *Pow-Wow* and of no real importance but the incident has proved your influence again. All the time I was supposed to be highly irritated you were listening in and saying, 'Is it worth it?' And of course it wasn't because the only thing worth any of it is you and all the fight would leave. By the way, you must know that we have an eleven o'clock rendezvous because some nights you're just there! Absolutely! Some nights I have to wait for you. Some nights you're doing something else and sometimes when I've been talking or thinking of anything else you call me—most decidedly. You're so very near all the time now—can't imagine what it will be like when you are really there.

21 November 1942

We've got a diphtheria epidemic. About thirty cases out at Middleton. Luckily, all so far are mild. About six weeks ago we had a malaria scare but that was soon under control. Let's hope this goes the same way. Oh—the JHC wanted to know what I meant by writing that the man who did all the circus props was our 'fairy godfather'. They felt certain it was impolite. Incidentally, Gurney and Devine who put out a men's paper were locked up for an hour because they had written that 'latest London news about our feathered friends'

(84)

was ... HC asked how they got London news. Was there a wireless? No! No wireless, that was meant to be funny. JHC didn't think it was funny and are still searching for the wireless. Wotta life! I want out!

29 November 1942

It's amazing that time spent so unpleasantly can pass so quickly. Less than a month till Christmas. How far away it seemed when we first came in. Have got over the periodic depression again—it comes every few months—and am sailing in a fairly smooth stream. See odd people but spend most time alone with you. Knit (still), write, practise Braille, and am now sewing a doll for the kids' Christmas. It was going to be a smallish clown but it has just run away with itself and become enormous. Must sacrifice an old pillow-case for its costume. Fun yesterday: out of the blue came a Louis Paul book about NY from the little tough Australian who helped Mrs Owens and me when she was evacuated from KL. Don't know how he knew my married name or that I hailed from NY. Frankly didn't think he could read. Very pleasant. On the whole Englishmen amaze me. I bake cakes for some and they return the tins empty—but two of them, nice ones too, return them unwashed. Do hope that you have two enamel mugs, darling. I got a second, sheer extravagance, the other day and it's done wonders to my morale. Do wish the blinking Sikhs wouldn't keep marching around sticking their noses into the cells. Between them and the Japs one can't safely wash or such until dark. Thank goodness they don't come around then. Been planning our home under any circumstances a great deal recently—think that no matter when or where the smaller the better. We don't need much room, just enough to have a place for everything, and it'll be much more fun. Oh, lots and lots of plans. Darling, I'm so glad you're you!

(85)

2 December 1942

Nine months today since we parted. God, how I hate this bloody existence!

8 December 1942

The rainy season has come with a vengeance. The corridor where I sleep and practically live is like the Grand Canal. Two nights ago I had to keep an umbrella up the whole time—very uncomfortable way to sleep. That green macintosh sheet is a godsend—one of my very best possessions. That and my chair and my lavatory brush. Still mourn the loss of typewriter. Local authorities say they are powerless, as it was confiscated by the Military Police. Am so full of writing it's nasty to have to borrow a machine all the time. Am down to some sketching too but that's depressing because can never do what I want. Wish Shellonizoff [the Russian artist who was living in Singapore] were here. Much ARP practising (just a year ago balloon went up)—rather amusing, for some days we aren't allowed to use the siren. All the laws of cause and effect seem to have been suspended. One never knows what is going to happen. The constant godsend is the speed with which the time passes. Food is not too bad when augmented by private purchase (Dunc a big help). Ethel's Red Cross shop brings in lots of stuff and she has been most useful in her tornado-like way. Only, of course, one never knows what's going to happen next. Katherine may be back this week. I like a number of people but she's the only one anywhere near like a friend. Spend most of my time with you. Recently too have had a reading jag which makes up for the months when I couldn't look at a book. And so we have December. Another flash and we'll be out and be together. Together, darling. Can you imagine it?

(86)

Darling, this place would have you in hysterics. You know the massive concrete walls, the solid, firm appearance—well, the rain comes through! Not through the roof or the little windows with their fascinating bars but right through the walls. Some of the cells are wet through. Luckily we're on the dry side. No place to spend these days but in the cells. How I hated them at first—now ours seems quite cosy (still hate it!). Sketch, read, plan and am genuinely amused. Ethel flirting with disaster again. Don't know what I'd do without her.

13 December 1942

Today, after ten months in this hole, discovered a window that looks right over the wall across to Selarang barracks and Changi. The former so close one can almost touch them. The owner of the window thinks I'm crazy—spent the day looking out alternately grinning and sniffing—never knew you were so close. Yesterday's achievements must be recorded—most mornings make a list of the things I'd like to or should do during the day. If by the evening I've polished off three of six feel fairly content. Yesterday finished the entire list and then some more, e.g. washed clothes, sewed bolster-cases (out of St John's apron,) ironed, picked a papaya, cleaned cell, embroidered name on remaining towels. Read and rested and thought up some inexpensive Christmas presents.

15 December 1942

Great excitement—men and women may meet for two hours on Christmas Day. Wives of course are thrilled. We're all thrilled but, gosh, why can't we even get a Christmas card to you? Elizabeth Ennis and I try to console each other. But we don't succeed very well—otherwise am having fun. The men are having another art exhibition next week. This camp is not very art conscious so just for devilment painted a surrealistic affair (hand holding candle, candle really female form, infinite sky, purple oblivion, mother earth, a toad, etc., etc.) showed it to a few here today and all called it, 'Very clever'. Most asked, 'What does it mean?' And all looked frightfully registering-intelligence. Apart from the fun am not satisfied—it's very badly painted. Maybe some day you'll see it. Katherine does not seem to be coming in for Christmas—if she does not return soon will have to share the cell with someone else— hateful prospect. In the meantime Ethel has nicely double-crossed Eleanor. Ugh—how much longer will this last?

20 December 1942

Delightful surprise today—Elizabeth Ennis had invited me to morning coffee. When I arrived found table all decorated and little presents. She said I had missed out on a bridal shower— so here it was. She remembered my saying that it was just two years ago today since the Sapper dance at Blakang Mati [at which Philip and I had our first date]. Have seen a lot of her lately and we are entertaining together on Christmas Day when the men come over. We're allowed to send you one present and a ten-word message. Perhaps the slippers will reach you? Please. Much excitement over the holiday arrangements. We live so much in purdah. I don't like the feeling—want you—badly. Christmas still means home and my parents and lots of grand memories. It seems all right not having those when you're about. But so—no like. Let's have lots of children and good Christmases of our own (even without lots of children). Sleep tight, darling.

26 December 1942

Philip, we were together yesterday. I can't write any more. Oh, Philip—my own. [Most of the Army wives had been allowed to meet their husbands for just half an hour outside the prison.]

30 December 1942

Have you managed to get over the thrill of it yet? It was so crazy—thirty-seven minutes in the sun outside my prison walls, and yet it was the first normal, real half-hour in the last ten months. When we're not together things don't count. Of course there were a score of things we did not discuss but when you held me in your arms it seemed as if nothing could separate us again. We were 'at home'. You looked very lean and gaunt and I am more worried than ever about your health. What fun it will be to feed you up. You said you were not bored—of course not, you could not be—I worry about your reaction to the damned futility—it's funny to think of you going in for languages in a big way—still wish you'd try carpentering, etc. You say you're good with your hands— I don't believe it—anyway you must develop into 'something useful round the house'. It's grand about your stories —please keep them safe. [Philip had never tried to write fiction but now he had finished two or three short stories. It did not become a habit.] Loved my presents—am in your pyjamas right now. Perhaps we will meet again soon. Look, darling, a whole page without blubbering! Take care of yourself, I love you so.

6 January 1943

Am still so full of talk with you that don't feel like writing.
Much fuss here with the coming of the New Year. Spent the
eve with Dorothy Cornelius who is still very worried about
her Bill [a Colonel who was in the Military Camp]. I have a
new cellmate, Olive Sowerby, Yorkshire nursing sister, and
very pleasant. Terrific camp row between Ethel and Eleanor
even affecting the Men's Camp. All most deplorable. I have a
new children's book on my mind. The thing is just running
away with itself. Don't feel like writing it but will have to try.
My yearning to get out and to you has become an absolute
obsession. Must shake out of it or another year here will really
get me down. (Then get worried for fear we mean so much to
each other that when we get out we won't be able to live up to
it all. Consolation is that even if I go wacky *de temps en temps*
you'll always retain your balance.)

10 January 1943

Fun last night—was a glamour girl in a show we were allowed
to give the men. Fourteen hundred packed themselves into the
front yard—how they did enjoy seeing women again. It was
grand to hear their applause but I am glad you weren't there.
Don't mind what we might have to go through together but
don't want to see you, nor have you see me, in such a filthy
position, separated. Even my overgrown sense of humour finds
it difficult. Felt it so strongly, gave the cell a helluva cleaning
today.

14 January 1943

Wow! Just been told that another two hundred and fifty women and children are coming—that means three to a cell. Ah, well, it also means Ruth Russell-Roberts [an old friend and the wife of Denis Russell-Roberts, an officer in the Military Camp. Ruth had left just before the fall of Singapore on a boat which we knew had been bombed] and goodness only knows who else. Must get things ready for her. Wonder whether Denis knows. Thought of Lynette's [the Russell-Roberts's daughter who was in England] birthday on the 6th (did you, godfather?). Wish Ruth Swann was there too.

16 January 1943

Can't get a moment's peace to write these days—everyone is so upset and flustered trying to make living arrangements. We, who were horrified at the idea of one human being living in these cells, now we have to live three in a hole. Nice and snug. However, what's a spot of discomfort more or less—it does mean more of us together (am told we are far better off than the Palembang crowd [an island where some of the survivors from the bombed boats were interned]). We do at least have running water, light, etc. (since last month there's a source of constant hot water as well) and the concrete is easy to keep clean. Food is bloody but sufficient. Some think the move a forerunner to repatriation—anything is possible. Today we filled out another pedigree form. About once a month we have to tell name, age, race, nationality, occupation, etc. What they do with the forms no one knows but they just love 'em. Very fond of new room-mate, Olive Sowerby, a very Yorkshire sister who was out only a few months when we capitulated. Her courageous commonsense and wit typifies the spirit of Britain. She too was horrified at the spirit of Malaya last

Jan.-Feb. Am glad—it was a dreadful disillusionment for me—many others here would not admit it. Oh, Philip, my boy, often wonder what battles we'll have to fight when this is over. They won't seem hard if we're together. In fact am looking forward to us licking the world and then some. If only we could start. In the meantime doggedly plod on with your green pullover.

6 February 1943
[My birthday and our wedding anniversay]

Good evening, mine, we've been so very much together all day it's silly to write about it. We've been so close it's hard to believe that you didn't really see the little parties and gifts— especially the lovely green housecoat that K made out of a bedspread. Am really getting quite a decent trousseau together. Olive gave me a very fine pair of white satin pants, Pauline D some good hankies, and then masses of Changi presents— coffee strainers from sisters' veils, odd tins of food, bumpf, home-made bridge scorers, etc. But this day must not take up too much space of this letter for I'll remember it all and in the meantime much has happened that needs recording. Mainly of course K's return. It was good to have her back—we get along so very well and it was grand to get all the messages from outside friends. They have been really wonderful (some even sent in little gifts for you).

7 February 1943

Just before K returned we were told that due to the shortage of space people would be allowed to live in the corridor where we had always illicitly slept and I had my official *Pow-Wow* office. I booked space for K and me, Kate and Olive took the

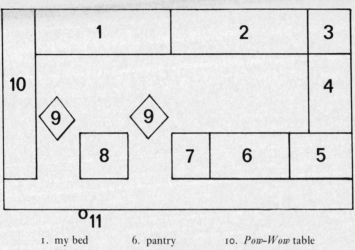

1. my bed
2. K's bed
3. frocks
4. shelves
5. shelves
6. pantry
7. scullery (basin and pail)
8. table
9. stools
10. *Pow-Wow* table
11. pipe leading to drain for toothbrushing

plot just below. This corridor, seven feet wide and about a hundred and twenty feet long, is separated from the big Carpenters' Shop (name of our only hall) by a grid and from the high wall that once separated the Asiatic and European quarters by (a) iron bars (b) a drain (c) ten feet of earth now almost a garden (usually hidden by rows and rows of laundry). Each corridor pioneer was allotted eight feet of corridor (two feet of width to be left free as a passage). I got an extra two feet for an office table. Pleased as Punch at getting what we had always wanted, K and I moved in. The move was an absolute circus (forty sq. feet does not mean much room) and we had collected so much junk that we dearly loved. Everything seemed to be everywhere, which would not have been so bad if there had not been a week of exceptionally high wind and our corridor acts as a funnel. Everything blew all over the place—other people's sheets appeared on our beds, our pots and pans rattled, coconuts rolled off the ledge and were eaten three stakes down. Our corridor was officially christened Hurricane Alley. K and I put on our looting specs and gathered in hessian, tin, sacks, tikah [matting], etc. Eventually we made ourselves fairly rain- and wind-proof and now we're quite shipshape. In fact it's very much like a cabin (next time we'll travel first class).

We do love our home and are plumb delighted to be out of the cell and away from the stairs, etc. Housekeeping is so much easier. You see, Philip, quite apart from the early rushing about and bluffing ourselves, there are now so many things that we want to do that we must regulate our chores to take up the minimum of time. Keeping our laundry, flat and body clean, redoing the blinking slops into a semblance of food, sewing the odd thing for the Men's Camp and also doing a Camp job, leave horribly few hours for important things. *Pow-Wow* is great fun but to impress people with my willingness to do 'my part' I clean a bathroom—thus get out of sitting on squabbling committees. This lavatory cleaning takes me five minutes a day and I put on a pained expression when I tell people about it. It's one of the best ramps I've discovered yet. K has caught on too and does a drain—this takes her ten-fifteen minutes. I'm trying to get her on to a nice five-minute lav. too. Having thus disposed of our duty to the Camp and to the simplest standards of hygiene and civilisation, we get on to what we like doing. Could write and write and write. Sometimes feel like sketching, occasionally like reading, rarely like knitting, at the moment am overwhelmed by a passion for poetry. Very lucky, have been able to get hold of a number of books—Keats, your Brooke, Carmen and Horey, Shakespeare, a 20th century anthology (good!). There are a number of good women in here and occasional conversations are food for thought. K came back converted to Christianity and a belief in the British Empire. We argue delightedly—each feeling that the other just won't see the truth. Kate preaches Buddhism and Middleton Murry, Marion—the *New Statesman*, Cicely—

(94)

child mortality statistics, Miss Sadler—the *Methodist Monthly* and Pauline writes music and uses broad 'As'—oh, yes, and Elizabeth Ennis recalls the words of Corral, her Girl Guide Leader. The news is good—it always is in Changi—Russia is doing well, North Africa is almost finished, Churchill and Roosevelt meet at Casablanca. The war will be over in three months, maybe three weeks or three years. A Nip gets tight and comes into the Camp at ten in the evening, does a bit of sloshing and goes away, much agitation, the racial question crops up again, more rows between the Committee and Red Cross factions, food is getting shorter, food is enough, we open a tin, the men are allowed over once a week to give a lecture (one man). The expected three hundred and fifty new internees do not arrive. Will they? When? Will it be hell? Won't it? Eighteen men come down from Penang—nothing but rice and vegetables, not even tea—solitary confinement until three months ago. Aren't we the lucky ones here in Changi. Oh, bloody well, yes. So we play bridge and mahjong. One of our pals is on the DI [Desperately Ill] list with dysentery—this is a very interesting experience, this is sanctuary, this is fun all right if you get out at the other end. We hope she does not die. This is no place for a finish. God, darling, how I want this to finish, to get out to you, to start living, together we can make an achievement out of life, this time is not lost if it makes us better equipped to do so.

12 February 1943

We had a most wonderful treat yesterday. The men were allowed over to give us a concert of classical music—Van Hiens really excellent choir with one outstanding soloist (Woods). Eisinger is easily the best pianist I have heard in years and Eber a satisfying violinist. The whole thing was perfect—that grand feeling of elation so rare in Changi jail.

Even the big Sikh guards tried to walk on tip-toe. The evening formed an unexpectedly good ending to a flat day. Wives and husbands within the walls were allowed to meet for an hour. All morning heard the bustle, saw the pretty frocks, smelled the perfumes, and later heard the men's voices. I consoled myself with the (sour grapes) thought, 'How glad I am that none of these men is my husband.' Also, 'How glad I am that my husband is in the Military Camp.' Pooey— I scrubbed my lavatory with a vengence. Just now K and I and three others are sitting under the one brightish light in the blacked-out building. In back of us is the now so familiar sound of people going up and down the iron stairs—a funny dull thump making an almost continuous drone, the background to all the other Changi noises. There has been much rain (Hurricane Alley was almost washed out—out flat was the driest of the lot) and tonight we cannot study the stars. They have become good friends. Oh—and tonight went to my first Mandarin lesson—it was quite good fun. Would prefer French but it's at such a beastly hour. Also Mandarin is more use if we stay out here and for many reasons that seems a good idea. Goodnight, my darling, sleep tight.

24 February 1943

This life is becoming more and more like a Marx Brothers film. Eleanor was told to resign—Cicely was elected head. Darned funny how the Camp is neatly split, Red Cross (Mulvany) versus The Rest. Politics wax hot and heavy and go as far as physical violence. The Camp was given about a hundred baby chicks and as many young ducks—even without the still-expected internees we are a bit overcrowded—so we got permission to walk within a restricted area outside the walls three times a week. Very nice too. Also a string quartet from the Men's Camp may come over once a week for an hour. Pleasant. We go for our monthly picnics to the sea and meet hundreds of Australians, we all are very pleased to see each other and wave and wink. The fact that we are heavily guarded by many Sikhs with guns and *lathis* and stopped every few hundred yards by Nips makes little impression— they seem our proper picnic companions. Also every Monday evening a man may come and lecture to us. Big Sikhs come with him—they look very fierce but when we laugh they laugh too though they can't possibly have understood. This is a helluva life but have become more reconciled by thinking that in war (as in life) everybody must play a part—either that of the soldier being killed, the wife waiting, the this or the that— well, we've been cast as prisoner-of-war now—we might as well play the part gracefully, though heaven knows I'll be glad to walk off stage and play wife to you—properly. Apart from separation this isn't too bad—now that we are settled in our Alley we can, with some organisation, get our chores done and have time for a few pleasures—but I intend to go at them without pressure. To hell with Mandarin—would rather write a bit, sketch a bit, do Braille and, what with bridge and chats, time flies. My need for you is so great that it takes all my energy to keep it from almost breaking me. It's a physical ache for your presence.

26 February 1943

That was going to be some deep thought before the ink ran out two days ago. Tonight will tell you some of my Changi ideas for our home. (1) Luggage must be light and made so that when not in use each case fits into the other. This saves storage space and drives the cockroaches mad. (2) If we're in London or somewhere where rooms are small and cupboard space restricted, instead of having one's box mattress on a bedstead with four legs, the foundation is an arrangement of

(97)

drawers (made of light wood—easily movable for cleaning) for holding shoes and winter or summer clothes depending on the season. (3) In our den, library, or what we'll call our room, the entire wall must be a huge map of the world—this would be very decorative but I love big globes (do you?) too—we'll have to decide. Have some other inventions but they are mostly cooking utensils—now I'll have to invent a way of making you make them! Am reading Middleton Murry—he annoys me.

27 February 1943

Forgot last night to tell you about our bedroom furniture—it won't be any of the usual pieces of furniture but all—

4 March 1943

Interrupted again, darn it, will wait and tell you about our bedroom furniture when we meet. Am feeling very good today; spurning internment, looking forward to the future and getting the most out of the present. Every Thursday morning K and I sunbathe. Today we were a bit harried, for dozens of men's fatigues appeared in all corners and we finally had to sit in a corner of the Infirm Ladies yard where the sun shone somewhat and we played piquet in our bathing suits. At eleven we had a cup of coffee, at twelve stood myself under a tap and now should be doing many things but feel like writing to you instead. Am very fond of Thursdays. Mondays, Tuesdays, Wednesdays am busy putting out *Pow-Wow*. Fridays wash and spring clean. Saturday have sketching lesson with Mrs Bateman. Sunday mornings we usually entertain. Tuesday, Thursday and Saturday evenings play bridge. Wednesday evening Shakespeare reading. Monday evening the men's lecture. Tea time these days K and I speak French (mine awful). Tuesday and Thursday afternoon Arts and Crafts classes, Monday and Friday afternoon—Braille with Miss Sherman. Every Saturday night Robbie, Eleanor and I have supper together. The week is highly organised but satisfactory, for it makes the time pass quickly. Day before yesterday it was a year since Fullerton. So far, so good. Even this life has had its moments. Lord, how one learns to savour every little thing that's good. How utterly unaffected one becomes by man's opinions, for one sees how unfounded all those opinions are. One loves humanity in the abstract and certain humans in particular—this love is the essence of living and how one learns to appreciate life. It's good, darling, terribly good—the few miles separating us seem unimportant. I feel so intensely, in fact I *know* we are *living* together.

Later the same day—gotta write some more—am getting such a kick out of life—the wackiness of it all—e.g. the war— such a heap of fuss and bother—everybody going hard at it, killing, destroying, hating and yet look at the haphazard way one gets (not even chooses) one's enemies and allies. Look at the way victories are determined. And then, I suppose we 'also serve who only sit and wait'—so we grumble about the food and ask for more communication with the outside world. Seriously again, I am often amazed at the hatred and loathing I can feel for individuals and their activities but I'll be darned if I can hate a race, nation or religion to order. Should I ever devote my life to a cause (apart from you) it would be to the breaking down of this damned national, racial and religious prejudice—war or no war. Fight for your ideals, die for your ideals but never forget what you're fighting and dying for.

7 March 1943

Having been lying in bed looking at your photograph. Really I could kick Mr Wong for taking out your wrinkles. Put them in once but you haven't got a glass and they've all been rubbed away again. And just now I want you—not the usual way but ... Don't like Othello as it is—it's not plausible but if I made Othello a Joe Louis, and Desdemona the spoiled daughter of Brabantio, the racehorse and stadium owner. That way it all makes sense. But I can't do it without you—haven't got the power nor the balance—it's got to be tough but not preciously so. Also my blank verse needs your pummelling. Have been playing with it quite a bit and everything fits in—it's fun— let's do it when we get together. Gold cigarette lighter with the cat's eye instead of the handkerchief. Shakespeare wouldn't mind.

21 March 1943

The past fortnight was very pleasant. K saw George, Marion saw Fred and I, at least, had news of you. With luck we will meet next month. The days passed with their usual Changi speed and we laughed a good deal at all the ridiculous situations. Then today, by an inconceivable chance, I saw K collapse into the drain she was cleaning. I was on the floor above and it took me some time to reach her—she had almost drowned in the few inches of water. It was a small stroke—she was still twitching when I got her out. Now she is in hospital and the doctors say there is no cause for worry. She still looks awful. Darling, it is the people one loves who make life worth living—I want to get out—not just out but out to you. The one person who has made Changi as easy as it is, is K. Why must there be all these horrible, sordid, unnecessary interruptions? One does not want much—one is willing to put in everything thank God I got there in time—it might have been so different. Darling mine, when will we have each other?

4 April 1943

Oh, sweet, the world is better today than it was at the last entry. K's seizure was due to worms, plus being run down, and now after various doses and ten days in hospital she's back again and life is more or less in its old tracks. I had a streak of dire depression. Since the Capitulation (more than before) I had banked my all on you, on being with you—as soon as possible. Then came the latest C [Churchill] speech and our reunion seemed further away than ever. For a while it seemed too far away to come true ever and there was no meaning in anything. But now it's worked out again—the longer it lasts the more I've got to pull through and be there ready for you at the end. I've got to make up for every rotten minute you've had as a POW. Now it seems so important that we meet and that you be convinced that at the end we've got so much, so very much, waiting for us. You never were very sure of me. If only I could know that now you have the certainty. Perhaps we'll meet on the 29th. During the past month $10 came from you. Philip keeping his wife. You need every penny and I hated the fact that you were able to send it but it did make a big warm feeling. Want to go shopping with you. On the 2nd we had a Fair Day and the camps mingled, K and I entertained Dunc, Cooley, Rock, Churchill, Ferguson, Salmond, Railes. All were very impressed with how civilised our corner was. We crowed with delight. Being civilised is our strongpoint—we've put up pictures, have flowers in bowls and use tablecloths. It's darned funny but we get a terrific kick out of it. How the internees have changed the jail—no longer all grey and bleak. We planted papayas and shrubs all over and built various huts—corners of it are not at all had now. To return to the speech, though personally depressing, it was generally magnificent. Here is something to fight for—with luck there won't be the same postwar muddle (there'll probably be another kind—seriously, though, it was inspiring). And to return once again to the depression, it was not alleviated by the thousands of letters that arrived and not one for me. No word from Mother for more then eighteen months. Wonder what the deuce she's up to! I'm very fond of her and she does do the darnedest things. Hope the postcards arrived. They are cads the way they kept us all bottled up with no news coming or going all this time. Schweizer and the International Red Cross were recognised a few days ago—that should make a change. Food, I hope—you looked very thin on Christmas Day. Conditions in town must be dreadful. Though the three hundred and fifty new internees never came, sprinklings of odds and ends arrived including three nuns. It's pathetically amusing seeing them trying to find an inch of privacy—what a time they must have washing their yards and yards of clothes. *Pow-Wow* was a year old last week. By the way, I've never mentioned what enormous pleasure I get out of the few pictures saved from the flat, the bits of jewellery and (don't laugh) your pyjamas (putting them on is the nearest thing to having your arms around me). Wonder in what you find your fun and solace? Do you think we'll ever stop talking when we do get together?

10 April 1943

Our hosts are in a devilish mood. No knowing what's going to happen next. Two days ago more than a hundred Jews were brought in to the Men's Camp—at a moment's notice, leaving their wives and families outside, just so. The men are almost distracted. Then most of our 'privileges' have been rescinded—no more Art Classes, no more men's lectures, we must speak Malay if not Nippon—to the authorities, oh, all sorts of little things. Goodness knows what's up. *Pow-Wow* hasn't come back from censorship yet; they're bound to object to something. In spite of all this, have been having a good time designing jewellery. Have a few most satisfying ideas—platinum ear sets and novel settings. Great fun. Repatriation rumours are high again—until it comes off, K and I remain busy planning at least one decent meal a day out of the gup and odd bits we can buy. Wish I could cook these suppers for you. (Oh, darling, so often think of your remark, 'Rationing wouldn't worry me except for butter.' 'And the King said, "I do like a little bit of butter with my bread."') What a ridiculous situation: either it kills you or you come out laughing. (Incidentally our pal got better but is still in san.—so is Lady Heath who, after being moribund for almost a year, returned day before yesterday looking better than almost anyone else in here.) Do you have parties with Denis RR and John Burns? Can hear the three of you laughing and cursing at all this. Gosh, darling, how I love you. Must stop writing or I'll slobber.

17 April 1943

Just read a letter from a woman in Australia whose husband and parents are here. She's living with an aunt who looks after her little girl and she works somewhere in an office and goes to night school twice a week and occasional flicks with other Malayan women. What an existence. This may be mouldy but at least it's positive—also rather amusing; our hosts are in a helluva temper and continue stopping all the privileges they ever allowed us, e.g. the bathing picnic. Last week's *Pow-Wow* was withheld completely—undesirable, too much levity, lack of food and clothing not to be joked about—also Mr

Tominago [the new head of the Camp] would not discuss the policy of the paper with me because I am a woman. This week's issue in mourning where they censored their own announcement that the Arts and Crafts Classes were disallowed. So? Life here very mixed: bad news of 'Ginger' Franks's death in Calcutta, and 'Bird' Nelson (Kathleen's husband) was carted off the other day with religious mania—a bloody situation. On the happier side we had a typical, swell party last night when Olive was on night duty (we always spend the first part with her). Maggie Webb made ice-cream in the refrig. (hospital) and opened a tin of, guess what, strawberries. Unfortunately, all the lights had fused earlier on so the ice cream wasn't set—but excellent all the same. There would have been a row if we had been caught in Matron's office at midnight, for Matron is one of many fusspots (we have about half a dozen Matrons and could do without) but Robbie is OC hospital and our pal. Great rumbling of lorries all night. Rumours of Changi moving—maybe you, too—nevertheless am still hoping for a meeting on the 29th and knit like fury on your green pullover, which reminds me that while I worked on the front, cockroaches ate three holes in the back. Darned now and practically invisible but cursed like a trooper. Repatriation still high—almost as high as this time last year. Oh, Philip—just worked out a great thought. Have for months, years, been painfully homesick for a glimpse of America—when you're demobbed let's blow ourselves to a real honeymoon—three to six months in the States—would you like that? We can always make more money and this would be such a good way of spending what we've got and you will need a holiday and we both need a honeymoon very badly. Don't you think it's a good idea?

20 April 1943

Oh, honey! Guess what—Brian Harrison had a letter from his mother and she's seen my mother and she's had our cable and all is grand and Mother must have met Daphne who knows you and now Mum will know all about us and I needn't worry any more. Golly, what a relief! Oh, let's get out of this soon. If I get out first am going to keep a full diary of all I find out about what's going on in the world for you. Will have to make up so much. Won't it be grand meeting people who have never even heard of Changi? People who don't think this is the be all and end all. Hopper [Eleanor Hopkinson's husband] sent over Beethoven's First Symphony this weekend. Like it. Especially the first and fourth movements, but the second would lend itself well to ballet. Oh, and Johns [head of the Men's Camp] is locked in a lavatory again (for telling a lie). Wotta funny life. Wonder whether you're still in Changi.

6 May 1943

More time gone, taking with it another Easter and Emperor's birthday in Changi. Our hosts' bad temper celebrated both occasions, solitary confinements, beatings, etc. I fear they do not like us. In the midst of all, Americans were called up. Repatriation or annihilation was the question. With trepidation we entered to be read, most ceremoniously, a telegram from the Secretary of State, Cordell Hull, saying we were not forgotten. Very nice, too. Since then American-born wives of Britishers have been asked to choose one or the other nationality. So now I am an official South African. I try to click and sound convincing. The day I heard from Mother was so elated that I let them put me up for the Entertainment Committee. Having kept out of things for a year, think it grand fun. Women do get so upset about anything—especially noise, yet each one wants to produce her own special music—result, constant rows about this as everything else. 'Swonderful. Have made *Pow-Wow* a bi-monthly. Still knitting your unending pullover. According to rumours we're going to be repatriated next week. Ever since we're in here we're going to be repatriated next week. I may be getting a typewriter—how I miss mine. Wonder where you are?

23 May 1943

Was fed up today so went to Church knowing that the Bishop was coming over. K spoke of him a great deal having been out at same time and seeing much of him. He was new to me—what he said was of little depth but how he said it was perfect. His voice, his manner, each gesture—all magnificent. John Hayter, a cherub of a man—the ideal curate, came with him. The two cheered me up considerably—in here everyone is so mediocre, so petty, unconstructive and unpolished. Outside there'll be the constant thrill of meeting people, any one of whom may turn out to be big. I like people who do things well. The Bish, with his Napoleonic air, 'bishes' well. It gave me new zest for life. The Camp remains incredible—for over a year the main clamour of the women has been to see their husbands—they have just been allowed fortnightly meetings. While our hosts were 'restless' they ordered all the men in from the ex-Sikh quarters, now called Golders Green. Cicely put up a suggestion that the large families be allowed to live in these houses and that the other marrieds take turns, week at a time, with the odd houses left over. Sounds a pleasant suggestion—no? But did it rouse controversy! The older and fatter the wives, the louder they proclaimed that they weren't going to spend a week with their husbands à la Brighton. What, prostitute themselves! Give the black and tans a chance to breed more brats (our children are not universally popular)!

Open mating season! Oh, you should have heard them. Many suggested kicking Cicely out for the infamous suggestion. Most of us just looked with open months, scratched our heads and wondered. Darling, I love the British. Also I am getting a typewriter. Also the food has improved considerably and we have received masses of presents each; four clothes pegs, sandalwood soap, one towel, four yards of material, toothpowder. Internment is becoming positively sissy.

5 June 1943

So many things have happened. On Monday evening we were told that Judy and all dogs (four this side, more with the men) had to be taken to the office next morning at 10.30 to be shot. This was awful. K and I ran around with a petition. Got all the children to sign and, by the grace of God and Tominago's good breakfast, got a reprieve for Judy and one other dog. It was a close shave. Very sorry about the others. On Tuesday we were allowed to send our third postcards home. On Wednesday they took away all electrical appliances from the Camp. Was sorry to see my iron go, it was well looted from the General. And then somehow in the middle of it all I found myself writing a scheme for the non-school hours of our children and now find myself in complete charge of the blighters (sixty-six of them) from 12.30 every day. Am really very fond of them and am enjoying the work and its organisation but the beginning is tough going. The women have all become very irritable and short-tempered and the children, lacking discipline, are naughty. However—K and I continue to get on very well. We congratulate ourselves on our flat and though this life is very wearing we try and generally succeed in not letting it get us down. Find much solace in my typewriter—a hulking big office Royal, but a typewriter. How much longer, darling?

29 June 1943

What busy full weeks these have been. Am thoroughly enjoying the children and they are reacting surprisingly well. They're funny little blighters, only about half a dozen pure Europeans, the rest all sorts of weird combinations. They now speak with a trace of American and I've picked up a number of words I didn't know before. They're just having a fortnight's holiday from school so I have them in the mornings as well as afternoons. Built a terrific path. Apart from the children there has been a great deal of internal political trouble. Cicely is out (a cigarette lighter was not handed in) and a most inefficient crew is now at the helm. Rumour has us out of here shortly (well, someday it must be true). Last week we had all our things searched. They took a candle from me but otherwise were very decent—considering the general atmosphere. Then we got permission to give the Circus to the men on 3rd July and that takes some rehearsing and preparing (it's the second show to go over). And on top of it all *Pow-Wow* is put out regularly—still quite some work, though I made it into a fortnightly about a month ago. The darned women won't contribute! However it all makes the time pass and keeps one out of most of the Camp squabbles which really are a bit over the odds these days. Would swop the whole blinking shoot of women for just one man—Philip, how I long for you.

20 July 1943

Well, darling, we've spent another of 'our days' apart—I had a TAB injection and in desperation ate a jar of olives that had been hoarded in case we had another meeting. Pooey! The Camp is really in an awful state and there are constant rows and bangup fights, with women landing in hospital. We have a very mixed crowd. K says we're now seeing life as it really is, without the veneer and polish. I don't like it. It was fun though giving the Circus to the men. How they did enjoy it. 'Twas really a success. Now back to quiet life again. Living so very much on top of one another peculiarly makes one enjoy one's own company more and more. Have made some handsome new cushion covers from a blackout shade, some dead shorts and the leftovers of my housecoat. The flat looks superb. Today's *Syonan* says repatriation is being arranged. The curse is a dreadful nuisance in this place, what with no privacy and no what-nots. Ah, well, we've done eighteen months now—surely that's more than half way, please!

22 July 1943

Forgot to tell you an amusing incident at beginning of month. Message came that the Nip Authorities wanted to see person who wrote *Pow-Wow* editorial right away. So I stuffed my pockets with bumpf, cigarettes, food and a book in case of solitary (not that I had written anything to warrant it but one never knew). Mr Tominago was all smiles (which I had been told was a very bad sign) that developed into chuckles. He thought the leader very funny, most Nipponese would not be amused but he was a man of the world. 'Were another Nipponese in charge it would be wiser not to treat serious subjects lightly. All very funny, though! Good evening.' So now we're all friends together and when he sees me with my eighty children I get an extra smile. Oh—might be able to see Duncan Wallace weekly because Helen is my cousin—would be fun.

6 August 1943

Julian Taylor [an outstanding surgeon in the Military Camp who was allowed to come over for consultation] was in day before yesterday. Reports of his conversation make the POWs much less comfortable than we. Oh, darling, my darned impotence in not being able to do anything for you makes me feel ready to burst. Our food has improved beyond recognition since the IRC [International Red Cross] stepped in—but you don't seem to have them and then you send half the money with which you might buy things to me and—oh, hell. The best news yet was Mussolini's retirement on the 27th July, though I personally think that Russia giving up parts of the Commintern some months back was of greater ultimate significance. If only the whole thing weren't so frightfully slow. The day we parted you said it would be a year and a half to two years and I resigned myself to that—now I hope you'll be right. Each day isn't so bad, it's just when you look at the whole collection of them that you get sick.

23 August 1943

Most of the cells in the Men's Camp have names—the other day four inmates were playing a quiet game of bridge when a very tight 'Blue Stocking' [a Japanese sergeant] barged in and knocked them for six. A few minutes after they regained their senses a big sign appeared over their door 'Pearl Harbour'. (Incidentally the drunk's migration landed about twenty men for hospital treatment and knocked almost a dozen women down or out—great excitement.) Then there was a cholera scare which got us all inoculated—do hope you had to undergo similar precautions. The day before yesterday Dr Lawrie, good chap from Penang, committed suicide. But in spite of these grim episodes the Camp is on its toes with the general news as good as one dare hope. I, darling, am in a complete state of the jitters. The idea of having this end and being with you is just so overwhelming that it frightens me. If the end is near (say within six to nine months) I sincerely hope repatriation gets beached and we return to a life here. Gosh, Philip, what enormous fun it would be. The damp weather is setting in again—how is your lumbago treating you? My, there's so much about you I've got to worry about. Must tell you: refereed a football match yesterday (took Pear's Encyclopaedia with me)—most unusual experience.

6 September 1943

Biggest news is that I've got two letters, that is I haven't got them yet but on the 2nd (eighteen months since Fullerton) was told that a batch had arrived and I was one of the lucky ones. Now they're being censored (as if that hadn't been done before) and I'm on tenterhooks. First news in all this time. Much talk of repatriation and IRC has been told to stop supplying us with food. (Well, it was good while it lasted). See Dunc for half an hour every other Monday. He is much better but if the women, children and sick go first he will be included. In meantime each day passes and there's never enough time to do all one wants: children, *Pow-Wow*, another art exhibition, Judy's on heat and needs special attention, dancing in a concert (polka day before yesterday big success), have written and am producing a sketch for the 25th, washed a blanket the other day and hands still a mess, K and I talk incessantly, try to rejuvenate our clothes, swop, mend, and devour all rumours avidly. Kate, Olive, K and I are one *kongsi* but Eleanor, Robbie, Cicely are always around. Pauline Dickinson and Rhona Dewe have been very good. Valerie and others come and go in spasms. Oh, and for a fortnight, I'm back at serving (shades of early jobs). Philip, I want to know

(111)

what you're doing and how and finally I want to do it with you. Take care of yourself, darling. Have a frightful urge to kiss you—just now.

17 September 1943

What a relief to have heard from Mother, though it makes one's blood boil to think that she has been all these months without any news. Why? Great excitement—rumour (with some basis) that the Americans are leaving end of this month. Don't know what I am according to Tokyo but don't want to leave unless we all go. Now meet Dunc weekly (and a pleasant change too) but what a situation when that's possible and I can't even write to you. Everything's crazy. One letter to Asian boy said, 'Hope the —— Japanese bastards are treating you well'; Japanese was crossed out by the censor and Nipponese put in. Also amusing story of Blue Stocking's having a tooth out. Then today I was called up again— objection to a poem in *Pow-Wow* by M. Thomas. They thought it was by Lady Thomas whom they are treating very badly but it was by Mary Thomas. All well. Don't know why they are so down on the ex-Gov's wife. Her greatest fault is that she's utterly and completely negative; has been no more use in here than she was outside. Most peculiar. Oh—and this month all the Army wives got double pay—why? Also letter arrived for Ruth. Some things one wants to forget about— never can. Cecil, writes Mother, had a daughter—back in Dublin. When will we be where? Also, have you read Shirer's *Berlin Diary*? Am finding it good reading—neutral, pre- judiced but not blindly and many insights I didn't know. Also good way of getting dates straight. Funny business in Italy now, isn't it? Be seeing you.

26 September 1943

Two days ago celebrated Mother's fifty-ninth birthday. Marion, Kate and Olive came to supper. I had tried to make an extra-special dish of coconut, sweet potato and peanuts and then to gild the lily had added some garlic. What a powerful mistake. Very annoyed that day because we had an art exhibition and our hosts commandeered all the pictures of Changi. K had done one of our corner (her only venture into art and jolly good too). I put in one I had done for you. It would have been a pity to have lost them. [In the middle of the night Katherine and I sneaked barefoot into the art exhibition, took our beloved pictures and replaced them with lesser works of art. We returned to our beds safely and utterly elated that we had done the Japs in the eye again.] Repatriation rumours still strong. I have bought yards of organdie and am filling the time making pyjama-, handkerchief-, etc., cases. Since I have only your pyjamas, practically no hankies, making very sissy, pretty containers is fun. Anyway, it's not sordid and that's a great change. G'night, darling.

13 October 1943

Great excitement. On Sunday morning we were told to have a roll call in the garden at 8.45 a.m. Last time it lasted half an hour. This time it ended at 7 p.m. Everything everywhere searched, scores of soldiers with fixed bayonets, no food, all privileges stopped. My things were gone through with a fine toothcomb, nothing taken and everybody very courteous. Eighteen men have been taken away. Goodness knows why. No one knows what they're hunting for—all very mysterious. And a new batch of letters arrived (four for me, whoops!) but they are not being censored until this schlemozzle dies down. Hope soon. And how are you keeping, Major Bloom?

* * *

Much has already been written about what came to be known as The Double Tenth (10 October 1943), the day the Japanese Kempe-Tai descended on the Civilian Internment Camp convinced that they would find an organised spy ring transmitting messages and organising sabotage on Singapore island. The fact that the accusations were without foundation did not prevent the imprisonment, torture and often death of a number of men (including the Bishop of Singapore) and a couple of women. After the war the perpetrators were tried and the worst offenders were executed.

On 00 October I was arrested and taken from *Changi. Years later back in England I wrote an account of what happened :*

The Germans had the Gestapo, the Russians the Ogpu and the Japanese the Kempe-Tai, brutal military police forces whose existence had only one justification. It is a warning to all of us just how thin our veneer of civilisation can be, how prone to bestiality we humans still are.

The Kempe-Tai in Singapore was informed of certain acts of sabotage in the harbour and elsewhere. They decided that this sabotage was organised from the Civilian Internment Camp and through radio transmitters. Having come to this decision, they then set out to collect confessions. The truth was irrelevant to them. Their aim was to send an impressive report back to Tokyo.

The Kempe-Tai headquarters had been set up in, of all inappropriate places, the former YMCA building. Since it was not large enough to house all their operations, they had various 'lock-ups' in other parts of the town.

On 10 October 1943, they swooped on the prison and picked up any suspects who attracted them. Certain outstanding figures in the civil service, church, legal or medical professions had a natural appeal. Then there were the lesser fry who were vulnerable because of jobs they happened to be doing. Ambulance drivers, engineers, seemed a suitable choice. About seventy men were taken out. Some, for no known reason, were then discarded and sent back. About fifty were kept. From these the Kempe-Tai then proceeded to try to extract confessions.

The methods employed were not delicate. Some were straightforward beatings. Others were more complicated and involved electricity, water and elaborate racks designed to inflict the greatest pain. Starvation, filth and general degradation formed a background against which the methods of persuasion were applied. Death sometimes resulted, but not always.

It will probably remain a permanently unsolved mystery why they chose me to be one of their guests, and why, later, they chose Dr Cicely Williams as another. They obviously had no great desire to kill us. They never even accused us of being implicated in their main 'plots' in any direct way. But there never seemed to be the slightest doubt in their minds that they wanted both of us in their investigations.

The day after the big search, they came down Hurricane Alley and ordered Katherine, or rather the woman who slept in that bed, pointing to hers, to go with them. I did not know of this until about half an hour later. It seemed a good idea to join her and so I packed one or two essentials in a shoulder bag, and went up to the office to insist that she should not be taken alone. By this time they had decided that they did not want her at all. It was me they were after. The tables were turned and now Katherine argued that she be permitted to accompany me. This they refused. Looking back, the situation was not without its humour.

I was transported into town in an elegant car, with a cultured interpreter sitting next to me. We stopped for a few minutes at the YMCA. What I saw and heard in the hall there was not reassuring, and I was glad when my interpreter returned and told me to get back into the car. It was not a long drive to the Smith Street lock-up. Any direct questions on my part were waved aside. I was taken into the outer office at Smith Street and the interpreter left. I never saw him again.

In the office the shoulder bag was taken from me, so were my hairpins and glasses and rings. The elastic in my knickers was removed. Hardly a word was spoken. From some other part of the building came shrieks and groans such as I had never heard before.

I was then taken through a door which led to a passage about four feet wide. On either side were large cells about ten feet by seventeen. Thick wooden bars, an inch and a half apart, ran the whole length of the passage. The floors of the cells were raised about a foot from the ground. Outside each cell, rows of shoes and *trompahs* [local wooden-soled sandals] were neatly ranged. There were fifteen pairs outside the cell on the left. I counted them while the sentry opened a little door which had been built into the wooden bars. It was only about four feet high and I had to duck to get through. He pushed me in and told me where to sit.

Two rows of men sat facing the bars. Their legs were crossed. Their hands folded in their laps. They hardly looked at me as I entered. Three or four were Europeans. One, Walter Curtis, I knew as a Camp interpreter, a charming and helpful man. The rest were Indians, Chinese, Eurasians. All sat quite still, their eyes looking straight ahead. The sentry bawled something at them before departing. Another armed sentry patrolled up and down the corridor, passing us every minute and a half.

I looked through the bars across into the cell facing us. Fifteen men looked back. I recognised the one facing me. He was a good-looking, young, blond chap called Perry. We had met in Penang, where he had worked for an import and export firm. His wife was very attractive. He caught my eye and winked. Then the hands in his lap gave the thumbs-up signal. The sentry continued his patrol. Outside the shrieks and groans continued.

Surreptitiously I looked around. The cell was quite bare and unfurnished. In one corner was a toilet, European but strangely different. It had no seat and instead of a chain or plug it had an ordinary tap from which the flow of water could be controlled. Ten feet up one wall was a small, barred window. In the centre of the ceiling was a large, bare, electric light. That was all.

We sat for several hours. My back began to hurt and I leaned against the wall. The sentry did not approve. He prodded me with his gun through the bars, and made several unpleasant remarks. We sat some more. Once there was a shuffling and tramping in the outer office. The door was opened and two Japanese, bare from the waist up, dragged in an unconscious figure. The little door in the cell opposite was opened. Two men rose and lifted the body. It was carefully laid in a corner. The two men sat down in their places again. The Japanese stayed a minute or two, to make certain nobody had ideas of tending the wounded man. Then they left and the sentry continued marching up and down.

During all this time men had risen, both in my cell and the cell opposite, and used the toilet in the corner. We had been sitting a long time. I caught the sentry's attention and tried to explain that I wanted to 'be excused'. He seemed to understand and told the guard in the outer office, who roared back in perfect English, 'If the woman wants to wash, drink or pass water, there is a WC in corner.' I continued to sit but eventually became aware not only of my own discomfort, but of that of all the men as well. It was extraordinary, but their sympathy was so strong I felt I had to break the tension for their sake as well as my own. As I got up and walked to the corner I could feel each of those men retire within himself in his effort to give me a privacy that was not there. And then we sat some more.

Perry and I perfected a way of communicating, by wiggling into a position where our eyes and knees were in line with a gap in the bars. We spelled letters out on our knees, when the guards could not notice. We became the official lines of communication between the two cells. This was useful occasionally, when those who had been questioned wanted others who had been mentioned at the interrogation to know what answers they had given. It also gave us something to do and a slight feeling of putting at least something over on our hosts.

There was no way of telling the time, but it must have been quite late in the evening, when there was a great clatter and a banging. A young Chinese conscript brought in a *tong* [bin] of rice, filled sixteen rusty tin dishes and slipped them into our cell. We ate with our fingers. The men then went to the WC and washed out the tins. I followed their example. Later, the Chinese boy returned with a bucket of steaming hot tea, no milk or sugar. We held out our tins and he filled them. Some of the tins had rusted through and the tea leaked out. The holes had to be plugged with fingers as one drank. The tea was hot and my fingers blistered. A short, broad, bearded Chinese looked up from his tin and saw what was happening. He finished his tea. Then without a word took my tin from me, covered the holes with his rough, strong, filthy hands, and held it for me to drink, gently, like a mother feeding a child. For the next five months he regularly performed this gallant service for me.

Later, the conscript took the tins away and we sat down in our accustomed positions. As it got dark the bright light was put on overhead, and black-out curtains were drawn over the little window. A different sentry was now patrolling up and down every ninety seconds. This did not stop night or day, and the light never went out. Eventually we were given orders to lie down on the wooden floor. Body stretched out next to body, sixteen in all in the cell seventeen feet by ten. From other parts of the building the agonised sounds continued. We lay down to sleep.

It would be wrong of me to give the impression that all the men, European and Asiatic, behaved heroically at all times. A few broke and behaved very badly. They had every justification for doing so. The miracle was that so many of them were able to muster such strength, courage, self-control and, as far as I was concerned, thoughtfulness.

In Smith Street I discovered nothing basically new. Certain ideas were convincingly confirmed. I saw just how debasing cruelty is to those who inflict it, and that the true dignity of man lies in his self-discipline, and has nothing whatever to do with status or authority. A third point somehow surprised me under these circumstances, though I accepted it under more normal conditions. It is that more important than his urge to survive, is Man's need to retain his vanity, pride, self-respect, ego, whatever you wish to call it. He will endure torture, he will face death, but he will not give up his belief in himself. Even those who collapsed under the strain still attempted self-justification. It was in this trait that I found the deepest pathos. Once one understands this basic vulnerability one has no option but to love and sympathise.

It would be wrong for me to try to reconstruct my emotions. I was intensely alive to the minutest detail of what was going on, but there was no fear as one normally knows it. There was not even horror. This situation had gone beyond any normal concepts of reality, of existence. It was easier for me to feel with my fellow cell-mates than to feel independently myself. They were human beings and I could understand them. The rest was outside all understanding.

For several weeks each day was to pass much like the last and much like the next. We sat immobile, cross-legged, facing each other. Perry and I would sign to each other. Sentries would march up and down. Three times a day the Chinese conscript would come with his *tong* of rice and bucket of tea. At regular intervals we would get up and walk to the WC in the corner. At night the light would go on and we would be told to lie down.

The only events that followed no set pattern were the dreaded visits of the interrogators. We could hear their arrival in the outer office and we would all sit, breathless, as they came into the corridor. They would stop in front of our cells and shout out the names of those wanted for questioning. The victims would get up, pass through the little cell doors, carefully put on their shoes or *trompahs* and then disappear. There was no way of knowing how they would come back, or whether they would come back at all.

People were called out at all times of the day or night. We

never knew which names would be called, when we might hear our own. My heart used to beat so loudly I was certain I would not hear if they did call mine.

This unceasing tension lasted for many weeks. The vigilance of the guards never slackened, and it was hard for us to exchange even a hasty whispered sentence. Towards the end of December, the pace of the entire investigation slackened, and we were able to relax a little and get to know each other better.

Some of the prisoners in our cell were only temporary lodgers. The majority stayed put. We developed a great knowledge and understanding of each other. I was given an opportunity to know men I would not have known otherwise, and I was allowed to know men under circumstances few other women have shared. I do not think that such experiences are essential for the development of a woman's character, but I do not, in retrospect, regret having gone through them.

It is still extremely difficult for me to write about this time. The irrational sadism of the Japanese defied description. At least two books have been written on the subject. One is the official report of the case and is called *The Double Tenth*. The other is *Destined Meeting* by Leslie Bell, which is concerned with Philip's and my war experiences. The latter naturally idealises my own part. Its factual details are correct. The chapters concerning the Kempe-Tai do not make pretty reading.

It is impossible for me to omit all details of atrocities in writing at least a short account of the people who shared the Kempe-Tai experience. They were worth writing about.

Walter Curtis had the advantage of speaking Japanese. He unselfishly used that advantage to the benefit of all of us, with a saint-like devotion and persistence. My personal reaction to organised religion has, from an early age, been negative, because there is so much humbug and hypocrisy attached to it. I have, however, a deep, sincere respect for all honest and consistent faith and worship, whatever it may be. Walter was a Roman Catholic convert. He believed in his religion and he lived according to it. Never in all those trying months was he anything but humble and selfless in his attitude towards all of us. He was a good man who risked, and received, many a beating in his efforts to improve our lot. The Japanese had allowed him to bring his Bible into the cell with him.

His wife and nine children had been evacuated to South Africa. He assured me that he was not worried about them, for St Joseph would look after them. When I suggested that he was 'preying on' rather than 'praying to' the saint, he calmly shook his head and said he knew he need not worry. Somehow I felt certain St Joseph would not let that man down.

It was Walter who thought up our Grace after meals. 'Thank God, we don't have to eat this lot again.'

The first few days there was a tall, handsome, worried-looking man in our cell. His name was Dr Stanley and he was tortured to death during the first week.

We had another young doctor in our cell, and a tough little red-headed engineer. They became close friends. The doctor was a pleasant chap, but after the first few months he found the going pretty hard. The Scot, who had as little charm or grace as any man I ever met, did a splendid job in supporting and building up his very much weaker partner. One could almost see him willing his own strength into the man.

There seemed to be an extraordinary supply of doctors in the cell. One was Chinese, highly intelligent, cultured and neurotic. He was frightened and could not understand our European attitude of trying to make the best of things. Our occasional levity he considered insane. Our feeble but unending attempts to thwart the Japanese, he considered mad invitations to disaster. He tried to avoid communication with us which was rather difficult when we were practically lying on top of one another and, at times when dysentery invaded the cell, almost sitting on top of each other as well.

I got only one glimpse of humour in the man, and that was when, added to everything else we had to bear, the WC broke down and started to overflow. We all watched, mesmerised, as the thing gurgled, belched and then vomited its contents into the cell. At that point, Dr Lim raised his eyebrows, shrugged his shoulders and giggled.

The last doctor was dear old Fowey Clark, a Eurasian, in his seventies, who had not the slightest idea why he had been plucked from his home. He took it all with extraordinary calm and philosophical good humour. He later died quite peacefully.

It was appropriate that one of our colleagues was an undertaker, an eighteen-year-old Eurasian lad, who had been brought up in his father's business. In later months, when it was easier to talk, he told me all about his work and made it sound very interesting. He felt hunger more acutely than most of us, and would try to counteract the pain by filling his belly with water. He was a great fan of Larry Adler's and when our sitting-at-attention routine was relaxed, spent hours playing an imaginary mouth organ, using Adler's well-known hand movements. His closest friend was a contemporary Chinese lad, who must have behaved well, for there is little to remember about him.

Then there was Francis, a splendid, tough little South Indian, who had worked for the Public Works Department and was an authority on plumbing. The Japanese did not impress him. If ever a man was master of his soul, it was Francis. We all respected him enormously.

A more sensitive soul was my particular Indian friend, Mahinder Singh, a tall, young, well-built Sikh. He was brought in the day after me and at first I did not recognise him. As a matter of fact, we all thought he was probably a stool pigeon planted by the Japs. We treated him accordingly. At night, the guard insisted that he sleep next to me, probably with the idea of degrading both of us. In the middle of the night, I woke when something moved inside my blouse. I sat up with a start, which woke the Sikh, who was only an inch away. I had instinctively grasped the moving object, which now jumped out and ran away. It was a mouse. I was horrified.

The bearded, ferocious-looking Sikh smiled reassuringly and patted my arm. '*Tid apa* (never mind), *memsahib*. Is only leedle mize.'

In the course of the months that followed, we tried to tame the mouse with grains of rice, but never succeeded. Mahinder and I became good friends, but we put on an act of great hostility in front of the Japs. It amused us.

Sikhs never cut their hair and have not only beards but thick long black tresses which they cleverly coil in a knot on top of their heads and keep in place with a small wooden comb. Normally this is covered by an elaborately wrapped turban. The latter had been removed but Mahinder had been allowed to retain his comb. Having watched me trying to tidy my hair with my fingers, he gallantly offered me his precious comb, and I was then allowed to use it whenever I wanted it. Despite hints and even direct requests, the others were not allowed to touch it.

Mahinder's English was strictly limited but uninhibited. Our conversations were delightful, for I often did not have the faintest idea what they were about. Once he gave me a long lecture on the wonderful fish-hunting in America, number one man, very fine, kick out British Raj, now number one city fish-hunting. It took me over an hour to work out that he was talking about Washington.

Once he announced, 'Indian women never wear buffaloes.' I assured him it was not the fashion in America either, but this he contradicted. In the end I discovered that he had been told that the English word for a grey flannel skirt was 'buffalo' and 'buffalo' all grey flannel skirts remained.

When we made plans for meeting after the war, he promised he would be wearing a fine shirt and turban, 'very silk, very butterfly'.

One night when the main beatings had stopped and there was a lull in special atrocities, Walter Curtis and I started playing the fool and everybody laughed and forgot, for a little, where we were. Mahinder sat back grinning, 'That was much pippippery.' I asked what he meant. Almost impatiently, that I should be such a fool, he explained. 'You know hockey game. One side win. Everybody shout, Pippippery, pippippery'. Three cheers, I understood what he meant.

Incidentally, it had been not at hockey but at football that we first met ... I remembered the occasion well. My horde of children back at Changi, had decided to have a game and I was to referee. Knowing nothing at all about the game, I went on the field with Pear's Encyclopaedia open at 'OUTDOOR SPORTS: Football', and hoped to pick up the finer points as we went along. A fatigue of men were building something at one end of the courtyard and a couple of Sikhs had come over as their guards. I was far too busy with the game and my book of rules to notice them.

In the course of the match I was surprised to hear a referee's whistle blowing at times. After a time, I realised that the children, who intelligently were paying no attention to me but getting on with their game, were getting what they needed from the whistle and that the whistle was in the mouth of a young Sikh guard. His position and dignity did not allow him to run up and down the pitch but he refereed most effectively and I was able to retire to read up more of the game. It was this same Sikh who now became my special baby. He was very young, innocent and kind. When I was ill he took his shirt off and put it over my shoulders. When he was ill, I washed his dirty pants. Friendships are built on a basis of such gestures.

We had one absolutely dreadful creature in the cell, depraved beyond belief. He too became my good friend. He was a Chinese drug addict, skinny, mis-shapen, and racked by a hollow cough that always ended in a series of spittings and splutterings. This revolting scarecrow had a wicked sense of humour and could often, with a short sentence, put things back into balance when we had been in danger of going awry. Once the Japs threw him some sticky brown gum, which he said was opium. He allowed me to sample a bit, which was very bitter. It seemed to give him pleasure. (Incidentally, as soon as peace was finally declared, this nasty piece of work was among the first to come into the Internment Camp and visit me with a basket of fruit and eggs. He remains my favourite dope fiend.)

Others, European and Asiatic, came and went, leaving little impression. Certain people one never forgets. Norman Coulson was one of these. He was a tall, craggy man from Newcastle-upon-Tyne. I had heard of him before as rather a forbidding man, who was concerned with the water supply and plumbing in Changi. He had a reputation for wanting to impose all sorts of silly-sounding regulations regarding the use of water. What I did not know was that he had been an engineer with the Public Works Department in Singapore, that he knew exactly what strain the pipes at Changi could take and that he foresaw what the consequences might be if our water supply ever failed. Nor had I known that he had gone out on every possible pretext begging, borrowing and stealing pipes, elbows and spare parts, so that we might cope with any eventuality. Francis had been his key contact man in this venture.

He was brought into the Kempe-Tai two days after me and accused of being one of the ringleaders in the sabotage plot. They tried to make him confess that he had worked a transmitter and they tried to make him implicate other men, both in the Camp and out, as having been his accomplices. When he was brought in he was clean and neat and strong-looking. He was in the cell barely an hour before we heard the shuffling and tramping that announced the entrance of the interrogators. They stopped in front of our cell and he was taken out. A few hours later he returned. His shirt was torn and his body bruised and sore. The first thing he did on entering was to wink at me and give the thumbs-up signal. I was not to worry.

During the next weeks they took him out every single day. Sometimes he was out all night. Occasionally he came back looking none the worse and we would grin at each other. Sometimes he was flung into the cell bleeding and green with pain.

It was perhaps a week after his arrival that they brought him back unconscious. Two of our men dragged him into a corner of the cell. I got up and washed his face and wounds. The sentry shouted and screamed in his usual way, but I was in no mood to listen to him. If he wanted to open the door, come in and knock me down, he could. The odd thing was he didn't. He raved and ranted for a while, prodded some innocents sitting near the bars with his gun and then shuffled off. Later I realised that I had won a victory. After that, whenever a man was brought in badly beaten, I was able to tend him, albeit in a lamentably inadequate way. The sentries still yelled but I paid no attention, and after a time they did not expect me to.

It did not matter what they did to Norman, they never broke him, and always on his return his main concern seemed to be for me. He told me much about his wife, who was a nursing sister, and about his daughter. I am certain that his remarkably kind attitude towards me was somehow evidence of his love for them.

During the months we were together, I spent many hours by his side. He was a deeply religious man and I would read to him from Walter's Bible. He knew the King James version and objected to some of the wording in this, to him, strange edition, but he would listen thoughtfully and be satisfied.

(127)

The first week in the cell, perhaps due to the shock, my menstrual period began. Walter Curtis explained my predicament to the guard. Nothing happened for several hours, and then a roll of shiny, crisp toilet paper was thrown to me. It was not exactly what I needed, but it was all I got. Two months later the 'Welfare Officer' handed me a packet of sanitary towels. The joke was that, due to shock and malnutrition, I did not need to use them for well over a year. They were invaluable, however, for dressing wounds.

Norman would watch as I unpicked them and used the gauze as bandages and the wadding to clean and dress his wounds. His eyes would smile as he grumbled, 'Never thought I'd have to use those things.'

Once, when he came back more dead than alive, he opened his stiff, bloodstained hands and gave me a grubby aspirin. He had actually requested and received it, in the middle of all that was going on, because he knew I had toothache. As long as the world can produce even only occasional men like Norman Coulson, it is not a bad thing to be a human being. He was taken from our cell two days before Christmas and I did not see him again.

There were a number of other wonderful men—Stanley Middlebrook, Hagger, Perry, Hugh Fraser, Clarke—a formidable list, most of whom died quite unnecessarily.

We lived so close to death that our attitude towards it changed. In some ways it became almost a friend who might come and help us escape. Occasionally, one felt that those who died were cheating. My personal fear was not of death, nor even of the torture. Just as my strength lay in Philip, so there too lay my panic. I was afraid they might bring Philip in. There was no reason for it, but there was no reason for my being there either, nor any of the others. I could stand this, but I could not stand his being there or seeing me in these circumstances.

Most of the men who had been brought in wore khaki, all

grew long beards and looked emaciated. It was difficult sometimes to tell them apart as they were hustled down the corridor or dumped unconscious outside the cell. With each one my heart stood still. Adrian Clarke was left lying outside our bars, almost at my feet, for a very long time. I did not know him but his build and colouring were very much like Philip's. When he eventually raised his head, and I could see his face, I sobbed with relief.

(Luckily, during all that time, Philip had no idea what was going on. When my signature did not appear on the receipt list of his monthly remittance, he made repeated enquiries and was eventually told that I was in Singapore Town with some other ladies, engaged in needlework and handicrafts.)

My own questioning was ludicrous. It was at least a fortnight before my name was called. It is quite impossible to remember or describe my sensations as I got up, put on my shoes and walked out. Two Japanese, one the interrogator, the other the interpreter, sat at a little table. I was kept standing. They asked various questions of identity and eventually confronted me with a nursery rhyme and a shopping list. They were so pleased with themselves, so self-important, as they demanded an explanation of these incriminating documents.

The shopping list contained a list of names and next to each was written either 1 k. GM or 2 k. GM or even 1½ k GM. The names were those of women in the Infirm Ladies' Annexe and the numbers and letters referred to the amount of *gula malacca* they wanted me to buy for them at the Camp stores. In Malaya goods were sold not by the pound but by the katty, a local measure of weight, hence the k. But our little Nip friends were certain all this had something to do with the wavelengths of a radio transmitter.

When I explained it to them, they did not seem to believe me, but neither did they torture me.

The nursery rhyme certainly looked more intriguing, because

it was in Braille. One of the teachers from the local St Nicholas School for the Blind was interned with us, and I learned that she hoped to get permission to send out books of Braille nursery rhymes to the children for Christmas. My Braille was very rusty because I had not used it since Evander and I, therefore, practised on the odd bits of paper, which were now ominously held in front of me. I gave my hosts an elementary lesson in how the six dots were arranged, and we laboriously worked out that Mary had a little lamb. Really!

After half an hour, I was taken back to the cell. The expressions on all the men's faces as their eyes searched my face, my hands and feet, had a strange intensity. Sometimes faces, hands and feet did not look so good. Mine were untouched. The strain went out of their backs and they all relaxed.

The Japanese never used any instruments of torture on me. Once, when I was taken out, one of the guards socked me on the jaw and sent me clear across the room, but it seemed to have been a purely impulsive action which we did not hold against each other.

The routine of our lives continued almost unchanged, until well after Christmas. The sentries marched up and down, names were called and people went out for questioning. Shouts, screams and groans rang through the building day and night. Three times a day food was dished out; sometimes it was plain rice, sometimes it contained a few shreds of meat or vegetables. Our eating tins became even rustier. We sat with our legs crossed, facing the bars. Perry and I continued signing to each other whenever Perry was fit enough to do so. We all developed scabies, and the bug bites became septic. The wounds of the tortured men stank, and so did everything else.

On Christmas Day, Walter gave me a little coloured holy picture, which he had kept in his Bible. Everybody wished everybody else the compliments of the season. Perry was taken out and beaten black and blue. When he returned, his swollen hand grasped the bar nearest to me to steady himself while he took off his *trompahs*. Slowly the hand slipped down the bar and deposited a minute packet. It was a sheet of toilet paper wrapped round a sliver of soap. That night I went to the toilet in the corner and washed my hair with the soap. Guy Webb, the young undertaker, gallantly handed me his shirt to dry my hair and the Sikh lent me his comb. That was Christmas 1943.

Early in the New Year the main tension seemed to relax gradually. Questionings were less frequent. The sentries, instead of patrolling up and down, lounged in the outer office. They no longer demanded that we sit in straight lines staring in front of us. We could rest our backs against the wall.

Every once in a while, the 'Welfare Officer' would appear and put the fear of God into us again. He was an officer, always meticulously dressed, with a thin, pinched face. He actually was supposed to be in charge of our welfare, but his ideas did not entirely correspond with ours. He was obsessed that we were concealing things on our persons. He would come right into the cell, search each inmate carefully and then if he found nothing, he would as often as not calmly and deliberately knock out any inmate who caught his fancy. He always went through my hair very carefully. I wished it had been with a fine tooth comb. We dreaded his visits.

Towards the end of January, Cicely was transferred to my cell and that was simply wonderful. It is hard to describe her. She is a woman considerably older than I but with something eternally girlish and innocent about her. She is a woman of tremendous ideals and enthusiasms. There is nothing blasé or cynical about her. She is a brilliant, dedicated doctor. Right through her life she will deliberately, and also inevitably, be a young woman determinedly doing what is right because that was the way she was brought up.

Even before the shared Kempe-Tai experiences, I liked her tremendously for her virtues, but sometimes felt like spanking her for being, what seemed to me, so completely unworldly and deliberately unselfish. I know she liked me too, but was often exasperated by what she considered my sophistication, and even cynicism. The answer lay very simply in the fact that we had led very different lives.

In the Kempe-Tai, each of us felt a strong protective urge towards the other. I knew that this was an experience far more difficult for her to bear emotionally than for me. Knowing this made me have all the more respect for her magnificent courage and self-control.

Being together made our lives far more tolerable. She had not been tortured either, but had witnessed the gradual physical destruction of men in her cell. She had learned to love men like Jackson and Yoxall, as I loved Coulson and Middlebrook and one or two others. We could talk to each other about these things, and talking to somebody who understood was a tremendous relief. Both of us had instinctively known that we had to keep up certain appearances for the sake of the men whose experiences we found unbearable to watch. It was not necessary to keep up any pretence with each other.

(Later, people sometimes told us that they just could not bear to hear of our experiences. We could understand exactly what they meant. Compassion is probably the key to man's finest potentialities. It is also the reason why it is easier to suffer intensely oneself, than to watch or just imagine others in agony.)

Cicely and I talked and talked and talked. Cicely had a good collection of poetry stored in her mind and I re-memorised many of my favourites, knowing full well that I would forget them again in a very short time, but the effort of memorising was a pleasant change. I have a good visual memory, and could sit in that cell and wander through familiar art galleries, savouring many pictures that I knew well. Though words are really my business, I do not remember them and was not the slightest bit surprised when Cicely recited a poem and then had to tell me that it was one which I myself had written. Deplorably, I actually liked it.

Mahinder did not take kindly to Cicely's arrival and steadfastly refused to let her use his comb, despite my broad hints. Cicely did not find him enchanting. It must be admitted that by the time she joined us, he was no longer a strong, handsome, young soldier-policeman, but a skinny, green-looking big boy, who basically wanted his mummy and had to make do with me instead.

We all looked a mess. Plants need sunshine and so do people. We all had a cheeselike appearance. Our hair was dull, dirty and colourless. It was also lousy. Our skins were revolting, being covered with scabies, septic sores and bug bites. Most of us were skin and bones, but others were already getting slightly puffed up with beriberi. I had one remaining physical vanity; my nails were beautifully mani-cured. Mahinder had, with patience and his bare hands, torn two slivers of wood from the floor boards. One was my cuticle stick, the other my nail brush. I carefully bit the nails of my fingers into shape, but was not so successful with my toenails, until Guy Webb, the undertaker, gallantly gave me one of his metal fly buttons which proved excellent for the operation. A small square of red cotton cloth from Francis's shirt (which had been torn in shreds during a beating) formed a dainty container for my manicure outfit. (I brought it home with me and it is in my dressing-table now.)

The sergeant on duty in the front office had been replaced by something very much more human and every few days he would let Cicely and me out of the cell to wash in the Japs' bathroom. This was usually filthy, but it seemed heaven on earth to us.

Three or four isolated incidents impressed themselves on my memory like clear, permanent photographs. One was the day Cicely and I found that somebody had used a copy of the

English language *Syonan Times* as toilet paper and then forgotten to pull the chain. It seemed an instinctive reflex action that both of us without a moment's thought or hesitation, pounced on the paper, washed it off and read the precious words. We were lucky ... they might have been advertisements. Instead they told of the action at Monte Casino and, though it was naturally angled from a Japanese point of view, it gave us some idea of where action was taking place. On our return to the cell, the news was quickly flashed across to Perry and we could almost feel it being passed from man to man and from cell to cell.

Two of the other mental snapshots concerned the Japanese themselves. The first was a typical, shortlegged, bespectacled, buck-toothed sentry, who patrolled the corridor during the worst times. Whenever he reached our cell he stopped and stared at me. I tried not to think what was in his mind. The patrolling and staring went on and on. Suddenly he put down his gun, stuck his hand in his pocket and shoved a piece of chocolate through the bars at me. The expression on his face never changed and he continued marching up and down. What added humour to the situation was that the chocolate was still wrapped in its original paper. It was part of Red Cross stores meant for us.

The other Japanese was one of the barrel-chested, Samurai type. He was shoved into the cell opposite ours for two or three days, early in November. None of us had any idea why he was there. His sole clothing was a thin loin cloth. He sat cross-legged with the other prisoners but two or three times rose and, in the space behind the sitting men, went through a prolonged mime of a traditional Japanese sword fight. It was all done in complete silence (except for the continuous gruesome noises off-stage), and formed an unforgettable picture. When he was eventually taken away, his escorts punched him hard two or three times before removing him.

Another vivid visual memory was a natural phenomenon

that happened once and once only, towards the end of our stay. The sun had risen but the Chinese conscript had forgotten his usual chore of drawing the black-out curtain. A thin sliver of light passed through into our cell. As if by magic, we suddenly had a perfect view of the street outside, complete in colour, reflected on our wall. Everything was upside down but we could see people walking, rickshaws rolling past, boys on bicycles and even a car or two. Everything looked so normal, even though it was wrong way up. We watched entranced. Then the curtain was drawn and our moving picture show vanished.

Beriberi does not hit you suddenly. Gradually one takes on a certain puffiness, which first becomes noticeable in the feet. Mine had taken on the pleasantly rounded appearance of those seen only in very young babies. Unfortunately, my ankles swelled in proportion and that was not as attractive, but this was hardly visible, as I was wearing slacks. Unfortunately the swelling began to increase rapidly and my otherwise emaciated body completely filled the slacks and bulged over the top. I was blowing up like an oddly-shaped balloon.

Moving became cumbersome and difficult. I was enormous and each step was an effort. It felt as if I were walking on a rubber mattress. Cicely knew the symptoms well, and became rather distressed. She knew the burden that all this weight was placing on my heart and was not surprised when, towards the middle of March, I collapsed completely.

Every minute of that time is still clear in my mind, but it has an odd, dreamlike quality. My body no longer seemed to have anything to do with me. I seemed to be outside myself watching the scene, interested but unperturbed. So much had happened that my imminent demise seemed just another event to be observed. It was very kind of the people in my cell to take so much interest. I wondered whether we would ever get out. If we did, I would get my ears pierced and have some gold earrings, plain ones. Philip would like those. We would have a home and live together. Perhaps we would have a toilet like the one in the corner, but we would keep it in the bathroom. The idea of removing the seat and having a tap instead of a flush was really quite practical. I wondered why there was so much commotion in the cell and was surprised to see two Japanese soldiers standing over me. One was the office sergeant, not a bad chap really. He held my hand. Rather ridiculous really. All right. Let's all shake hands and be friends.

They brought me coffee, hot, strong, sweet coffee. Very nice too. Were they serving it to everybody? Cicely had removed my slacks and wrapped me up in Katherine's sarong, which I had packed in the shoulder bag. It was very kind of her. And then I slept a long time.

Two days later, I had another heart attack. The extraordinary Japanese seemed very upset. They brought in not only black coffee, but a little box of Vitamin B pills and they gave Cicely a long lecture on how rare they were. She fed them to me, and within twenty-four hours the swelling had gone down a bit. I was no longer so lightheaded and could move about a bit.

On 24 March, five months after my arrival, the Japanese called me out to the front office. The conversation was short.

Jap Officer: 'You are not well.'

I: 'This is not a healthy place.'

Jap Officer: 'We are very kind. We will see you do not die. Do you want to go to Myako Hospital for treatment, or back to Changi Internment Camp?'

I: 'I want to go home ... to Changi ... with the others. All of us together. Go back.'

Jap Officer: 'Very well. We will attend to it.'

I did not believe a word he said, though I wanted to so much. I did not know what to tell the others in the cell when they asked me what had happened. We had spent so much time trying to build up each others' hopes that, in this particular field, we no longer trusted each other. We could but wait and see.

The next day they came and called out just over a dozen names. From our cell the Scottish engineer, the young doctor, Cicely and I, were called. Walter Curtis, Hugh Fraser and the others waited in vain. They assured us we were not to worry; this was just the start; all would be out soon. Then we would have a party. They smiled and said goodbye.

In the office, we were officially and efficiently handed everything that had been taken from us. I was given the shoulder bag, my glasses, hairpins and even the elastic from my knickers. I had squeezed myself back into the slacks, but had to carry my shoes.

We were put in an open lorry, and driven back to Changi. That drive was remarkable for only one thing. We hardly talked. All of us were speechless with the sensual delight of looking at things in the distance. For months we had been able to see no further than the cell opposite us. Now we could look down a street, across a field and up at the sky. Everything was too beautiful for words.

*　　　*　　　*

19 April 1944

On the 22 October I was arrested and taken away from Changi. The following day Dr Cicely Williams was brought out too. On the 25 March we were returned under orders to say nothing. I am glad to be back. If two women had to be taken I am glad, I suppose, that it was us, for C is a *very* fine person and I am at my best when things are worst, but really, darling, don't want any more adventures—please, please start taking care of me soon (and for goodness' sake, try to steer clear of trouble yourself—not, it seems, that one can do much one way or the other). Our welcome here was wonderful; for once the whole Camp seemed unanimous in its kindness. Katherine is, as always, a gem and we are back in our funny little flat. Being a celebrity was embarrassing (Cicely took it most graciously—like Queen Alexandra on Rose Day) but it has died down. Now I sit back, beautify my face with your Christmas present, read and reread Mother's letters (she has met people who knew you and is becoming most enthusiastic), look at your pictures, dream and pray that this whole damn business will soon be over. How I long for you!

28 May 1944

Darling, the past few weeks I have been so happy that I'm afraid that sounds silly in internment, but then my bargain was made—separation gladly for the price of your safety in a world gone mad (as normal worlds will) and the bargain must be kept, cheerfully. The happiness is due to knowing you are well (you looked so young, so thin, strong, so you!). [Very occasionally parties from the Military Camp worked in the fields outside the jail. Sometimes stones, tins, bits of wood were used to spell out names—Smith, Jones, whatever it might be. A wife or girlfriend would rush to a cell at the top of the jail, climb up, gaze through the bars of the high windows and wave. It wasn't much but it was very satisfying. I had been helped up when 'Bloom' was spelt out some days before.] There has been further post from Mother, more victims of The Case have returned and I am out of jail. Please God you'll never be stuck behind those grey walls and bars. I hated them—every single minute. About a month ago we were told to expect good news, most thought it was repatriation and were very disappointed when it was only a move to Sime Road [another Military Camp from which the soldiers had been evacuated to join the main body]. Katherine and I are entranced; we have a corner in a hut apart from most others. The space in front just asked to be made into a garden and I spend my days in a delighted orgy of digging, watering, planting and wallowing through jungly paths hunting for flowers and ferns. Cicely is next to us; also delighted. (We are still thin but otherwise quite recovered.) Judy leaps through the tall grass like a rabbit. If only we could see the war out to its end here, with food, etc. no worse, to have you come and collect me, or perhaps I meet you in Changi, or perhaps— every evening I dream some new way in which we'll finally get together. Keep well, my love. There is so much for us to enjoy as one!

18 June 1944

Yesterday K's birthday and a great success. Delighted. She has been so good to me that any way in which I can make her happy is a find. Past weeks have been full, too full for a real account. Will just put down headings and give you the details when, some day, we sit together and you dip into this. There have been: gardens, septic feet, Iraquis, Eleanor going sour, Bach going hermaphrodite, Meyer Grand, Phil Tankard, Vyvyan Frampton, rats stealing buns, congested quarters for

most, we in clover, malaria, dysentery, wireless messages
(twenty-five words) sent today, made-to-order happy family
photographs, broken vegetable garden, the new General,
isolated graves, piquet, *Tristram Shandy*, devilish children, no
outside news at all.

8 July 1944

Yesterday was our day; we were very very close and enjoyed
the ridiculous full moon together. K had a small surprise
celebration, more or less to make up for the holidays I'd
missed outside. Cracked our last tin of cheese. Very good too.
Food here improved but I'm still tied up with these damn
septic feet, but don't pay much attention to them—been doing
more sketches but not at all satisfied with results. Last few
weeks the atmosphere has been definitely one of waiting. No
longer that awful Changi feeling that things will never ever
end. Rumours have been most optimistic and not too silly.
After Italy I expected events to move more quickly—wrong
again. Now am convinced that 1945 will see the end. The
attitude of our hosts has shown a definite improvement. Much
relieved—no one knew which way the cat would jump.
Garden doing well, 'relatives' meeting pleasant break, so are
weekly concerts. Remind me to tell you how we got Blue
Stocking's signature and how we saved the 'virtue' of the lady
in the Horse Box. Want to tell you soon, soon, soon.

18 July 1944

This morning I went to Norman Coulson's funeral service.
They brought him back dead yesterday. He was a very fine
person. Stanley is dead too, that makes two out of the four
who were out at the start together—and Walter is not back

yet. It was not a pretty show. Still surprised to find myself out of it alive. Darling, we must do something for Norman's wife and daughter—they are in Cape Town. Am so very sorry he's gone—it wasn't necessary.

30 July 1944

These weeks are difficult. A week after Norman, Hugh Fraser died. That's seven so far (and still sixteen out). Having seen them come out healthy, having lived in the same cell, sharing the same horrors, becoming friends, makes it all very hard. And still being tied up with septic feet leaves one too much time to think. Need you badly. Sometimes one is frightened for no reason at all. And there is no end in view. And—but, my darling, clasp you close and know we'll see it out. There is much ahead of us. Much to be done. To fill the days am going to teach the 6th and 7th Standards beginning tomorrow. The time must pass.

11 August 1944

Yesterday a good day—postcard from Mother dated 30 September 1943—cheerful and well. Monthly money from you with your signature—oh, how good it was to see the mark underneath your precious scroll. Stood over the list mooning like a lovesick schoolgirl. Teaching is proving much more fun than anticipated. Rumours are better than ever but how reliable can be gauged from the fact that I was told most confidentially that Roosevelt had been re-elected fourth time—and our elections aren't until November! Jo English, over at our recent births (Asiatics who were interned last Christmas—no wall-climbing!), was asked how he was, 'Very well but weak—so weak that in a forceps case the baby would probably pull me in.' Bowyer still out and the only one for whom I have no sympathy. A nasty piece of work! Kate coming down today to rejoin our *kongsi*. Really amazing how well K and I still get on. She unbelievably good, also good fun.

3 September 1944

Philip, dear, if you want to have a good-tempered, bearable wife don't ever let me write or paint. Will never be able to do either well and it makes me so darned irritable.

30 September 1944

This life continues to be one mad paradox. The General has just been round and most affably complimented me on my paintings (as a matter of fact he's not a bad guy), yet two more 'Case' people have died. All my years as a child used to longingly read of Southern children chewing sugar cane. For first time in life am munching a bit. Very good too but there's a new outbreak of dysentery. We are getting absolutely no news of the outside world, yet everyone is convinced that Germany is finished (oh, that it may be so!). Repatriation rumours rise and fall. Have made a bet with Dunc that we'll still be interned next Ides of March. Last Sunday celebrated Mother's sixtieth birthday. The garden is really lovely now. Remind me to tell you story of Rosita sending coffee and milk to her husband. Wish to goodness I were psychic—then might believe in my so very strong feeling that this is the home stretch and that it won't be long till we're together. Can sense it in every bone darling and it's good, so good.

Hot day. Just had a shower, the sun on the water made rainbows on my body and that was fun. But these days cannot take even such simple pleasures without thinking, 'Very nice but not what I want.' The urge to start life with you is so uncontrollably strong that it colours every minute of my days. Have learned a great deal during these two and a half years and some of the things will stand us in good stead but all I want, my only reason for living, is to get together with you. Middlebrook died yesterday. Another worthwhile person. I am not underestimating myself when I say that it would have been a better thing for me and some of the others to go than Middy, and Coulson and Adrian Clarke (ten in all now). You are the one thing that makes my life valuable. This is written not to be part of a love letter but an indication of how these months pass: chores, worry, pleasure in thoughts. So that's quite enough introspection—you probably know it all already. Wonder how this time will have altered you? 'Twill be interesting. The fundamental you will be the same but my poor Philip in surroundings so alien to his nature is bound to have some new facets. Feel quite drunk with anticipation, soon, soon, soon, soon!

16 December 1944

Do wish this book were longer. There have been so many thoughts and experiences I wanted to share with you that had to be shelved. At present am all enthusiastic planning a six-week domestic science course to start mid-January. If we're out before it's over won't grumble but feel these weeks must be filled—well! Have learned one thing—that both time and money are one's servants and not the other way about. If one really wants to do anything it can be managed. Our honeymoon in America will come off—we'll make it! And we can start children on our way. Used to worry about how and where you'd start again after this long break and whether you'd mind not reaching the heights you would have attained normally. Now know you won't. Whatever happens you're a darn good doctor and we're going to have lots of fun together. Know that the happiest marriages are those where the wife thinks the husband perfect and lets him know it. I don't think you're perfect and I can't make-believe but I think you rather wonderful and the only man for me. That, plus all the things we enjoy doing together, feeling together, thinking together— oh, my darling it should be pretty good and if there's not so much worldly success, who cares? We'll envy no one. So now on with Christmas (damned bore), on with preparing lectures for next term and on with peace. (PS More grand cards from Mother. Her love will add to our happiness.)

17 January 1945

Darling, know you are well. To hell with anything else. As a matter of fact life not too bad at moment. There have been a few good raids. Christmas went off very well in spite of a bad beginning, with Dunc's TB breaking out again and Long being executed [John Long was shot by the Kempe-Tai during the time of the Double Tenth]. The school has been put off for a bit as our 'Hall' has become a rice store and I want to write poetry instead of teaching. The phase will pass but just now think in blank verse and can't stop. Just re-read bits of this diary—awful! It's mental shorthand and won't convey it's true meaning to anyone (that is you).

Well, it's over three years now since the débâcle. Also we
have been married more than three years. That of course is
doggone funny. Also doggone satisfying—not the length of
time but the fact that we have each other. Looking about, a
number of things are satisfying—our planes in the sky—what
a difference they have made to the spirit of the Camp. Cooley
came to see Ena Farrer and was like a kid. This is going to be a
disjointed entry so might as well let it rip. End of January (20)
Mrs Graham White died. 6 February wonderful celebration—
room a bower of flowers. Surprise party by my girls and rest
of day one party after another (what a change after last year—
that was pretty grim). Following day your money arrived. K
and I bought *gula malacca* and coffee. Last week internees told
to hand in everything over $100. Speculation (mental and
financial) in great swing. This week Ethel has gone completely
off her rocker again—very upsetting. Food cut but K and I
very fit. Gardening like mad. Matron Stewart rioting because
we all use hospital ovens too much. Wonderful orgies of
surreptitiously cooked meals (tapioca and occasional eggs—K
and I make breakfast curries). Hooch (yeast culture, *bubor*
[sloppy, boiled rice] and sugar) drink of the day. Nagara [the
current Camp head] has his nose cut. Eleanor antagonising
whole Camp. Judy hairless but a great pet. Lady Heath goes
on night duty (she's most friendly disposed towards me once
again). Sylvia Tilley talks horses and turns this into *école
pour jeunes filles bien élevées* in her Ruth Draper conversations.
Simone Weinberg, charming and French, Mme Simpson
ditto. My French frightful but getting good airing. Endless
piquet. Marie Webster drives Kate dotty. Tense feeling that
anything might happen any day now—'slong enough—by now
Allies should be capable of preparing terms that Europe would
be able to take (wonder what the civil state of Germany is like
now!). Oh, Philip, won't it be exciting to get out and see

what's happening and what has happened? Do you think we will ever be able to take it all in? No matter what the circumstances we're going to find life wonderfully good.

5 April 1945

Germany must be the most capitulated country in history. Since we've been interned we've heard of her caving in at least a dozen times. She's done it again. Feel it might be true any day now. Last fortnight the number of female internees has more than doubled, with the Jews' wives and families (quite incredible) and Eurasians. All very cheery but you can't imagine present conditions. K collapsed last month, was nursed at home for three weeks then, as there was no great improvement, into hospital for a fortnight, now back looking better but still very weak. She just overdid things. Am very relieved that she is no longer in hospital, as the new internees' arrival coincided with a dysentery and malaria epidemic. News: all money was declared and anything over $100 was called in. The jewellery had to be declared; everyone very frightened but they offered to buy (I'd already sold most of mine). Much commotion about orders to sew for Nip soldiers. So far there are enough voluntary workers (getting extra food and pay) but if we're here much longer we may have to get down to it. Red Cross parcels arrived, promises of delivery before Easter (last Sunday) but so far just promises. As food has been cut and cut those parcels are pretty welcome. It would be the second delivery in more than three years. Admirable! On 25 March celebrated anniversary of return. It's good to be alive and am amazingly fit. Ditto most 'returnees' who survived at all. Ethel very bats. Am still convinced that a few months will see us out and with that pleasant thought leave you for today.

17 April 1945

The Red Cross parcels are not being given to us (after having been promised). Instead, they killed Judy yesterday. At an incredible interview they told us that the food shortage made it essential that none should be wasted on pets. It's silly but all the tears that I didn't shed for Norman, Middy and the sad state of the world during the last three years have now rushed out. It's all so inhuman, so evil. Have been doing much poetry. I feel that so much that is written is just pretty words—paper roses and sickly sweet scent out of bottles. Am trying to get at the essence of thoughts and emotions and express them musically but most simply. Occasionally succeed. Am most anxious to hear your opinion. K is better. Am not teaching but working on Camp gardens and hate every sweet potato. Skies quiet. Feel next six weeks should bring something.

11 May 1945

Red Cross parcels handed out St George's Day (that also Elizabeth Musa's birthday—all very jolly). Atmosphere incredible. Would give anything to know what happened at the San Francisco Conference. Also, now that Europe's finished, will Russia wave big stick in effort to secure negotiated peace out East or does she prefer to have us fight it out now that she's no longer in the arena? Gosh, Philip, it's all so interesting am just sizzling inside. Rumours grow more fantastic and contradictory every minute but the possibility remains—we *might* be together before the end of the month. This is undoubtedly the most unbearable time of internment.

15 May 1945

Philip, the realisation that Germany is really finished and peace is, if not reigning, at least declared in Europe, is so colossal I find it almost impossible to carry on with the routine here. If we settle in England, how about the coast between Folkestone and Rye (Dungeness?). We could live modestly but have a boat and a car and be equidistant between London and France? Physically I can do all sorts of things I couldn't do before internment—you'll find me much more use on a boat. And though we'll want lots of luxury we'll be able to contrive to get it simply. Honey, we're going to start life together soon. (Oh, at some point, let's visit the Scilly Isles.)

11 June 1945

Extraordinary life these days—feeling that at any minute they might sign and our troops arrive. In the meantime more parcels which makes a great difference to the body and morale, not that the latter isn't pretty good anyhow. Have become garden-ticker-offer—pleasant work. Oh, how I want this to end. Just bursting.

23 June 1945

Still here and more in the dark than usual. Hosts very bad-tempered; we optimistic—don't know cause for either. Swopped the beauty milk you gave me for a tin of milk—had been keeping it to make body beautiful for reunion. Internal beauty will be as important. Externally this sojourn has not improved me. Inside feel much better—stronger, younger, and would not have been elsewhere (that is if we had to be separated). Hope you feel the same. Occasionally get stagefright at thought of meeting but mostly it just seems as if a necessary part that is missing will be joined to make the whole. Camp news: Ethel no longer violent, K had her fourth birthday in internment, more Red Cross parcels were shared and food generally is a bit better. John and Dunc good fun on Sundays (Dr Reid Tweedy joined too). To make the end pass more quickly am mixing more in Camp. Good deal of French (Simone Weinberg, Mrs Simpson) and German (Petra Wajsmel, Stella Getreuer) spoken and some bad Malay (especially Fatima Jellany), off painting and writing. Today lights and water off; imagine it's something to do with the Tunnel which is causing so much speculation. [The Japanese General, commanding Singapore, had announced that regardless of decisions made elsewhere he would never surrender. Tunnels were being built all over the island, presumably as cover for his troops.] Oh, and wonder why for two months your name was on a separate sheet for monthly payments.

20 July 1945

Griffith-Jones has been off work leaving me as Head Gardener. Very amusing. Crisis—no veg. for women because of tapioca thefts (meant no lunch). Iraquis indignant. Everybody reduced (officially) to one suitcase, bed and stool— suits me. Haven't any more. Been having fun swopping things. Roll-calls on again. Not been a bad year so far because each week is so full of hope (if little else). But, oh, for one's own bathroom, food for which one need not queue, clothes that fit and just some privacy. What will it be like to lie in bed and not be heard by at least thirty people if one turns round? Rumours of more mail. Good!

5 August 1945

No letters for me. Life here increasingly irritating as the end comes nearer (what sort of an end, I wonder). Everybody hideously skinny and many of the older people giving in. It might be horribly depressing if it didn't seem almost inevitable that Singapore be attacked or Japan surrender shortly. On the whole the mortality rate has been wonderfully low. During past weeks I have mended a bucket with latex and canvas, produced footwear out of a defunct football, sewn endless garments with thread pulled out of a sock, cooked most satisfying concoctions from incredible things (we eat most of our flowers. K is most successful with chillies, tapioca—illegal—can be made into almost anything—good, too.) Feel capable of tackling any sort of life. Don't know how much of the news is true but the European political situation seems to be solving itself nicely. Labour Government in England is essential now and has come late enough not to be associated only with radicals, ruffians and upstarts. Blum, in France, has always been philosophically in harmony with the present trend and is impractical enough to accept any reconstruction committee's edicts. Of the new American President I know nothing, which seems silly. I am satisfied that regardless of what mistakes will be made (and must be made) they are on the right track with a common aim of international welfare and the strength of will to sacrifice old and dear traditions and sentiments to the general good. I cannot know but I feel that this war was worth fighting (one had one's doubts) and that when we get out we'll find a world worth living in—not as it was after 1918. Am so doggone curious to hear what you want to do. Anything, anywhere! Long time ago wrote a silly poem about 'My husband's my favourite man.' That was after we were parted only a little while. The more I think about it, the more I hear about and see other men (not much chance of the last—still get beaten if caught talking) the more those sentiments stand. What will happen when you actually have your arms around me and I look into those very dear brown eyes and we stand free, in this best of all possible worlds? ... Combustion, darling, spontaneous combustion. Will stop this letter. Should anything interesting occur may jot it down in blank pages in front of book. Otherwise no more until we meet.

21 August 1945

Your card arrived this noon! First rumours of peace hit us on the 11th—confirmation gradually trickling in—still nothing official from our Nips. Will you come tomorrow? Before the week is out? I am waiting.

Epilogue to a Diary

There never was any official notice that our war was over. Peace trickled in gradually. Some of our hosts faded away. Those who stayed rarely appeared and one or two actually tried to ingratiate themselves with us. Red Cross stores were released. Letters that had been held up were distributed. Then, one beautiful day, a small squad of super-men in red berets came to the Camp. They were some of Mountbatten's commandos. Each seemed ten feet tall, tanned, bursting with strength and unlike anything we had seen in years.

It was confirmed that the Japanese Emperor had surrendered. The General in charge of his forces in Singapore had, however, decided that he would fight on because his honour demanded it. It was tricky because the island was still covered with thousands and thousands of Japanese troops. We were told to stay where we were until the situation had clarified.

This was a sensible idea but it did not suit me. It was urgent that I see Philip and that he see me before anybody else told him about my Kempe-Tai sojourn. So one day in the last week of August, Katherine and I put on our very best dresses which we had saved for just such an occasion, and with John Dobie (Katherine's nephew who had been with the police), we crawled under the barbed wire and out of the Camp.

With studied *sang froid*, as if it were the most natural thing in the world, we hailed taxi and told him to drive us to the Changi POW Camp. The Chinese driver eyed us with amazement, smiled from ear to ear and drove off. His cab had been through the war too. It rattled like a cement mixer and had no springs but it got us there. The driver waited for us at the gate, having been assured of payment in good old Straits

(152)

dollars. These too had been kept for such an occasion. Actually, I have no doubt that he would have taken us just for the satisfaction of it.

At Changi gates, John left us. The man on duty, whose mouth had opened in disbelief when we appeared, controlled himself long enough to tell us that the hospital was at the end of the avenue to the left. The last we saw of him, his mouth was still open. Katherine and I started the long walk.

That walk became memorable. Men in shorts were working or lounging everywhere. As we made our way, first one and then another would come up to us, look hard, and then shake our hands saying, 'First white woman in three and a half years.'

The first time it was touching. The second and third just a little less so. After we had shaken hands for the umpteenth time, it was hard to control our mirth. Each said exactly the same words in exactly the same way. We knew that we must not let them down. Since we *were* the first white women in three and a half years, we had to behave appropriately but it was difficult to assess just what appropriate was. Not giggles, for sure.

At the hospital, Katherine quickly found George who was laid low with his old stomach ulcer. Philip was not there and nobody knew where he might be. Then somebody remembered that he had gone to see Allen Glendinning, an old friend. They rushed off to fetch him and I was taken to the room he shared with half a dozen other doctors. His bed was pointed out to me.

Up to this point, I had been in perfect control and had even been able to exchange a spot of snappy badinage with a couple of Red Berets who were surprised to see me and asked from where I had 'dropped'. Now, there I was, standing at the foot of Philip's camp bed. He had a sheet on it. The sheet was clean but it was old and had been mended many times, mended with different coloured threads in the most incompetent cobbling stitches. Typically Philip I looked at that sheet and began to sob.

Then he came in and put his arms round me. I buried my head in his chest and sobbed all over him.

We spent an hour together and then Katherine, John and I met at the gate and, in our rickety taxi, we returned to Sime Road. Our mission had been accomplished.

No matter what anyone told Philip now, he knew I was all in one piece. Katherine had seen George. John Dobie had met some of his Service counterparts and exchanged intelligence. Our taxi driver would be able to feed his family for a month and regale his pals with stories of the trip for a life-time. Not a bad day's work.

The following days passed slowly and uneventfully with one great exception, when Service husbands were driven over in lorries for a reunion with their wives. Philip and I quickly detached ourselves and, once again, hailed a taxi. This time we drove to my dear old flat in Chatsworth Road to see if anything was left but it had been stripped. Then we drove to see Goh Sai Poh and her family. She had risked her life repeatedly to send food and gifts in to me. This time, as we were leaving, she took us to an old carved camphor wood chest, opened it and said, 'Take what you want. You must need some money.' It was filled with Straits dollars. It was a gesture on her part that nobody has matched before or since. Goh Sai Poh and Kok Kee now live in one of Singapore's handsomest houses. He has retired from a distinguished medical career and she has been honoured internationally for her work in Family Planning in the Far East. Their son, Heng Leong, is a leading barrister in Singapore. We meet when we can. When friendship is so old and firm and tested, it creates a kinship. They are 'family'.

But I am running ahead of myself.

The one thing that Philip and I wanted most was to be together, alone. We looked forward to the trip home. Early in

(154)

September, we were told that we would be sailing on the first boat out, the *Monowai*. Marvellous!

When we got on board, she turned out to be a very old troop carrier. Katherine and I and about a dozen other Service wives were in one cabin. Philip and a covey of majors were in another, nowhere near ours. We had to meet on the upper deck. This was not the way we had planned it. I was beginning to learn that nothing ever is.

We almost had a mutiny on board because some well-meaning oaf had ordained that only soft, easily digestible food should be served to the returning prisoners who would not be able to cope with anything more solid. The returning prisoners had other ideas. They had had a bellyful of pap and wanted real food. After two or three days with ever-rising tempers, Philip, as senior medical man aboard, had a session with the Captain and the meals improved.

We had several hundred men and a few women on board. All were emaciated, tense and fed up with the way they were being treated. I never learned what the officers and crew of the *Monowai* would have preferred to do but they made it clear that repatriating ex-POWs to England was a confounded nuisance. They should not have let themselves be caught in the first place. It was not a happy ship as we steamed into Colombo harbour with everybody up on deck to see our first port of call.

The harbour was beautiful and it was obviously a holiday. There were hundreds of little boats, as well as big steamers, and all were covered with flags and bunting and making happy noises with whistles and sirens. On shore, church bells rang and there was a throbbing background noise as if all the cars in the town were hooting. Everybody on board was curious to know what the celebration was. Slowly the message reached us. It was a welcome. The whole of Colombo was saying 'hello' to us. Several hundred skinny men and a handful of skinny women grinned and stood up straight.

The Red Cross and allied services had laid on a wonderful welfare machine. We landed, were served a sumptuous tea and then went through a large hall where there were dozens of stalls. At each one we helped ourselves to whatever we needed: toilet bag, toothbrush, toothpaste, soap, nail brush, dressing gown, night gown (I got a huge flowered flannel affair which was later cut into dresses for our baby daughter), bra, cotton stockings (silk and nylon were war luxuries and unobtainable), shoes, skirt, blouse, cardigan, coat, canvas suitcase. They had thought of everything.

The men were given what they needed and new tropical uniforms. If my memory serves me, they were given their winter outfits later when we stopped at Tewfik.

Colombo remains unforgettable. After our windfall, some of us were invited to Government House. Sir Henry and Lady Moore welcomed us with warm hospitality. Sinhalese servants in spotless uniforms served delicacies on regal china. It was wonderfully civilised. We purred.

Philip found time to send a telegram to a Park Lane hotel booking a suite for our return. We were going to celebrate.

The *Monowai* stopped for a short time at Tewfik on the Suez Canal and then she raced to England. We were the first ship to land at Liverpool with Far Eastern prisoners of war. Excellent arrangements had been made for the returning, if not conquering, heroes. There was only one hitch. Nobody had mentioned that there were women on board. Pandemonium! What to do with us?

It was almost midnight when they took all the Service couples to a hostel that had been cleared. There were not enough rooms for each couple to have one. Again husbands and wives were separated. Philip and I had had enough of that and we decided to spend what remained of the night sitting in the lounge. So did another pair, Colonel Bill Cornelius and his wife, Dorothy. They were considerably older than we were, had been married for many years and were comfortable with each other. They wanted to be together, too.

When all the others had left, the lady warden twittered up to Philip and me and whispered that we should follow her. She took us up to the attic which had been turned into a dormitory with about twenty beds in it. She said we might stay there ... together. She made it sound positively naughty. We thanked her, looked at all the beds, hooted with joy and then went down to collect Bill and Dorothy.

And so our first, long dreamed of night together in England was spent in a Liverpool attic with umpteen beds separating us from the colonel and his lady.

By then, we had received a telegram from the hotel in Park Lane informing us that they were fully booked and could not accommodate us. It did not matter. We were together and the next day we made our way to London ... and a new life.

*   *   *

Even today, people still ask whether I hate the Japanese. The answer is and was, 'No.' I hate violence, greed, sadism, stupidity, arrogance, intolerance, ruthlessness. They are abhorrent no matter where they appear. The Japanese never had a monopoly on them.

When my children were five or six years old (yes, the fortune teller's prediction came true; we had a son and a daughter) they went to a little school that had dancing classes and, once a year, the school held a display. While my daughter was committing incredible *pas de chats* with other galumphing contemporaries, I was asked to hold two smaller children who obediently cuddled up on my lap. When my eyes strayed from my beloved offspring and I looked at them, I saw they were Japanese. They were little, innocent, trusting, vulnerable and as attractive as all children. Was I supposed to hate them because they were Japanese? I never met their parents. Perhaps, without knowing it, I made a point of not doing so.

Rationally, I have no prejudice. Emotionally, I am not sure but I think not.

As to Philip and me ... of course, we did not always come up to each other's expectations. Who could? We needed each other and tried to meet each other's needs. Having shared Singapore was a strong bond. Over the years, we have faced our share of storms and have come out weather-beaten but intact. Our children, William and Virginia, have added greatly to the richness of our lives.

The friendships made in camp were firm. Katherine and George settled in Jersey. We saw each other whenever we could, wrote letters and telephoned. Katherine died in 1979. She was a fine person and dear to me. I miss her. The DeMoubrays, like the Gohs, are 'family'.

So is Cicely Williams. She has continued her good work in preventative paediatric medicine and is still at it, despite the fact that her years should make her a very old lady. She pays no attention to that. I love her.

Kate Clark is retired, living in London and we have long gabfests when we can. An ever-increasing number of us have died. Others keep in touch. Being an 'old lag' is a strong tie, stronger than any old school tie.

The events of war-torn Singapore happened a long time ago. In many ways, I find it hard to identify with them. They now seem almost like something I read about in a book. Perhaps it was in a diary?